Mothering and Ambivalence

Parenting, lone motherhood and the breakdown of the family are all subjects of current political and social debate in the west, and there is little agreement among cultural commentators on what mothers should be, what children need, and how those needs conflict with the needs of parents. Feminists have played a large part in these debates in recent years, reacting particularly to negative portrayals of lone mothers in the press and the implication that they are the source of other social problems.

Mothering and Ambivalence brings together authors from therapeutic, academic and social work backgrounds to address these issues, but counters the reluctance of current feminist literature to embrace psychoanalytic understandings of dependency, anxiety and identity. Drawing on extensive professional experience, the contributors critically use psychoanalysis to go beyond the often simplistic claims of the political debate on mothering. In their discussions of parenting and gender relations within families, the authors also surmount the narrowness of purely feminist polemics, keeping in view the importance of the diverse identities for women who become mothers.

For all who are frustrated with the polarised debate about women's and children's needs and rights, this book offers an intersubjective approach to the emotional life of mothers, examining what it feels like to mother amid the pressures of contemporary social life.

Wendy Hollway is Reader in Gender Relations at the University of Leeds. **Brid Featherstone** is Lecturer in Social Work at the University of Bradford.

Contributors: Joanna Best; Ros Coward; Sheila Ernst; Brid Featherstone; Stephen Frosh; Wendy Hollway; Paddy Maynes; Susie Orbach; Caroline Owens; Rozsika Parker.

Mothering and Ambivalence

Edited by Wendy Hollway and Brid Featherstone

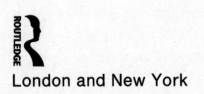

London and New York

First published 1997
by Routledge
11 New Fetter Lane, London EC4P 4EE

Simultaneously published in the USA and Canada
by Routledge
29 West 35th Street, New York, NY 10001

Typeset in Times by Pure Tech India Ltd, Pondicherry
Printed and bound in Great Britain by Mackays of Chatham, Kent

British Library Cataloguing in Publication Data
A catalogue record for this book is available from the British Library

Library of Congress Cataloguing in Publication Data
A catalogue record for this book has been requested

ISBN 0–415–13910–4 (hbk)
          0–415–13911–2 (pbk)

To my daughter, Ella, who I love best in the world.

W.H.

To my mother, sister and niece.

B.F.

Contents

Notes on contributors

Joanna Best works at the Islington Women's Counselling Centre as a counsellor with women in violent situations, and as a student counsellor at the London School of Economics.

Ros Coward is a columnist for *The Guardian* and Senior Research Fellow at Nene College, Northampton. She is the author of, among other things, *Female Desire* and *Our Treacherous Hearts: Why Women Let Men Get their Way*.

Sheila Ernst is a group analyst who worked for many years at the Women's Therapy Centre in London. She is in private practice with the Group Analytic Network in northeast London, teaches at the Institute of Group Analysis and in the Counselling Section at Birkbeck College, London.

Brid Featherstone is Lecturer in Social Work in the Department of Applied Social Studies at the University of Bradford and has previously worked as a social worker and a manager in the area of child protection. She is currently completing a PhD on the subject of women's violence towards their children and is co-editor of *Violence and Gender Relations*.

Stephen Frosh is Reader in Psychoanalytical Psychology at Birkbeck College, University of London, and Consultant Clinical Psychologist at the Tavistock Clinic, London. He is the author of *Sexual Difference: Masculinity and Psychoanalysis*, and co-editor of *Psychoanalysis in Contexts*.

Wendy Hollway is Reader in Gender Relations in the Department of Psychology, University of Leeds. She has researched and published on questions to do with subjectivity, gender, sexuality, the history of work psychology and gender relations in organisations.

Paddy Maynes is Clinical Director of the Islington Women's Counselling Centre. She has published a number of papers and articles on mental health issues for Irish women.

Susie Orbach has a long-standing interest in mothering as a daughter, a mother and as a psychotherapist. Much of her work has looked at the centrality of mother/daughter relationships and the problems surrounding the development of female subjectivity.

Caroline Owens is a child psychotherapist in training at the Tavistock Clinic with a background in psychiatric social work.

Rozsika Parker is a psychoanalytic psychotherapist in practice in London. She is the author of *Torn in Two: The Experience of Maternal Ambivalence* and *The Subversive Stitch: Embroidery and the Making of the Feminine.*

Chapter 1

Introduction
Crisis in the western family

Brid Featherstone

Western cultural commentators appear to be preoccupied with how children are coping with changing family forms. They are worrying about what kind of future generation is being created; whether mothers' and fathers' claims to personal rights are undermining their responsibilities as parents; what is happening to men; how the crisis in masculinity is affecting boys; what it means to be a father; whether women can really have it all – motherhood, sexuality and a career; whether women still need men.

In this book we address these themes, using and developing insights from feminist psychoanalysis about mothering, fathering and gender relations in families, and also about needs and desires, dependencies and jealousies, anxiety and identity. We also use psychoanalysis to expose the unconscious dynamics which motivate political positions in this area – feminist positions as well as others. Children's needs, for example, are understood by all of us through the prism of our own gendered and familial desires and identities. The idea of mothering in particular arouses anxieties which may be managed through defences which, reproduced at a cultural level, are manifested in the idealisation and denigration of mothers – neither set of images faithful to reality. Much of the British feminist literature on mothering is characterised by antipathy to psychoanalytic understandings and a related unwillingness to address the psychic difficulties men, women and children experience in changing patterns of gender relations, of parenting and work, and the resulting political implications. Here, we are trying to redress that balance.

Faced with the recent onslaught against any alternatives to the traditional nuclear family, especially if they involve women's independence from men, the danger is that feminism will concentrate so fixedly on opposing that backlash that we will not address the widespread anxieties about what happens to children when parental care fails. To stress the importance of child-care facilities for working mothers and to ask rhetorically why fathers are not being held equally responsible when children suffer is necessary, but it is not sufficient.

For example, in her widely publicised book *What about Us? An Open Letter to the Mothers Feminism Forgot* (1995), Maureen Freely argued that feminists have been concerned only with the needs of 'women' and not with the needs of mothers or children. This may be interpreted as part of a backlash against feminism, but could also be viewed as opening up possibilities for feminism to reframe the politics of mothering.

As Stacey (1986) warned in relation to similar developments in the United States, disagreements among feminists provided clues to gaps and difficulties in feminist thinking and to areas of pain and conflict in women's lives. In particular, she warned that feminists in the USA had relied too much upon voluntaristic strategies in relation to men and children, which led them to misconstrue the difficulties involved in constructing loving, egalitarian relations, and in meeting the needs for, and of, children.

A glance at the history of feminist writings on mothering bears out the difficulties feminists have with questions about women's and children's needs and rights. The role of men in relation to women and children also continues to be a lightning rod for tensions within feminism, and current debates on men's relationships with children after separation or divorce indicate that there are two positions emerging. One emphasises well-resourced mediation facilities and constructing and supporting good fathering practices (see Orbach, Chapter 6). The other highlights the vulnerability of women and children to violence and abuse when men keep in contact with their children (Hester and Radford 1996).

In the next sections the book's contribution will be located within feminist debates on mothering, on women's and children's needs and on the role of fathers and fathering.

CHANGING LIVES IN CHANGING WORLDS

Second-wave feminism's early texts were highly critical of the role mothering played in women's oppression (see, for example, Firestone 1970). They can be understood as a challenge to familialism, post-war idealisation of domesticity and a form of psychoanalytic thinking which seemed to prioritise children's needs (Everingham 1994). If the objectives of 1960s' and 1970s' feminism were equality and greater personal autonomy for women, mothering was seen as the greatest obstacle to this:

> The claim that mothers had rights and needs of their own provided a standard by which to assess psychological theories of child development. Feminist writers used this standard to highlight the innumerable ways in which psychological theories and models of child development oppressed women, through their failure to consider the mother's separate set of needs and interests.
>
> (Everingham 1994: 3)

In this period, 'To be a person, for the most part, meant to be a person like a man... Personness and subjectivity necessitated moving beyond, or avoiding altogether, home and motherhood' (Bassin, Honey and Mahrer Kaplan 1994: 6).

For Snitow (1992), this was the period of what became known as 'the demon texts' (for example, Friedan's *The Feminine Mystique* (1963) and Firestone's *The Dialectic of Sex* (1970)), which were accused of mother-hating. They were patriarchy-hating rather than mother-hating, according to Snitow, but they were limited in that they failed to speak the daily life of the mother. From a British perspective, Segal (1995) argues that the early period exposed many women's silent sorrow at home. The stress, isolation and economic dependence of full-time mothers was explored, for example, in Oakley's (1974) study of housewives. However, as bell hooks (1984) has pointed out, the specific circumstances of white middle-class women's domestic isolation were mistaken, in many key texts, for the universal, thus occluding whole swathes of experience of work, poverty and racism.

A flowering of feminist work on mothering followed, initiating what Snitow called the second period. In the USA, 1976 saw the publication of works by Rich, Dinnerstein and Lazarre. For Snitow, this period opened up a key political question which still remains unanswered: What construction of motherhood is most helpful for feminism? If we follow Dinnerstein, we are trying to get men to mother; if we follow Rich, we are trying to build a female culture. This lack of clarity about the goals of feminism where mothering is concerned continues to have grave political consequences.

Chodorow and Contratto (1989) argue that many of the writings of this time reflected culturally held beliefs in the all-powerful mother; idealisation and blaming being two sides of this belief. These writings have an unprocessed quality in which infantile fantasy has become confused with the actuality of maternal behaviour:

> Feminists take issue with the notion that a mother can be perfect in the here and now, given male dominance, lack of equality in marriage, and inadequate resources and support, but the fantasy of the perfect mother remains: If current limitations on mothers were eliminated mothers would know naturally how to be good.
>
> (Chodorow and Contratto 1989: 90)

Chodorow's *The Reproduction of Mothering* (1978) is itself a product of this period. Along with Dinnerstein's *The Rocking of the Cradle and the Ruling of the World* (1976) and an early article by Flax (1978), it laid the groundwork for a blossoming of feminist psychoanalytic work in the USA. This work, later often called feminist object relations theory, emphasised the importance of the pre-Oedipal period, in particular the mother–daughter relationship, the persistence of infantile ties and the effects of women's mothering on gender-based social relations (Bassin, Honey and Mahrer Kaplan 1994: 7).

The impact of this work in the UK was both theoretical and practical. The London Women's Therapy Centre was the first to provide both a service and a focus for the ongoing development of feminist psychoanalytic work in the British context (see, for example, Ernst and Maguire 1987). However, because of a widespread antipathy to psychoanalysis, women's studies and feminist work in the social sciences remained largely unaffected, continuing to approach mothering in a socially determinist vein.

According to Snitow (1992), a third period in feminist thinking on motherhood was ushered in with the publication of Ruddick's article 'Maternal Thinking' (1980). This, Snitow claimed, really ended the taboo on speaking the life of the mother. Ruddick has gone on to argue (synthesised in *Maternal Thinking: Towards a Politics of Peace* 1989), that children's demands for preservation, growth and social acceptability constitute maternal work and that to be a mother is to be committed to meeting these demands by practices of preservative love, nurturance and training. Conceptually and historically, preservation is pre-eminent in shaping mothering and it is neither historically nor culturally specific, unlike for example, the expectation that mothers should foster children's growth. Ruddick argued that, although the idea of fostering children's growth is culturally and historically specific, this does not mean that children's needs are primarily a cultural creation. She was clear that maternal work could be carried out by men as well as women. In engaging with the relation between mothering and what children need, Ruddick's work, though not in a psychoanalytic tradition, is a helpful model for this book.

However, the complexity of her insights became lost, alongside many others, in the polarised and politicised climate of the USA in the 1980s, where the politics of the family and relations between men and women moved centre-stage. High profile pro-family feminists such as Elshtain (1981) emerged, who charged feminism with demeaning motherhood and argued for the affirmation of family life as the locus of humanisation:

> Mothers were demeaned under the guise of "liberating" them. In many early feminist accounts, mothering was portrayed as a condition of terminal, psychological and social decay, total self-abnegation, physical deterioration, and absence of self-respect. Women, already victims of an image that denigrated their social identity under the terms of the male American success ethos, now found themselves assaulted by the very group that would liberate them.
>
> (Elshtain 1981: 333–4)

Writers from a variety of perspectives began to reassert a naturalistic view of mothering. The following wave of maternalism, hitched to the bandwagon of pro-natalism, fostered the valorising of motherhood as the site of women's moral superiority over men (Segal 1995).

Stacey (1986) argued that the emergence in the USA of conservative pro-family feminism in the 1980s resulted from weaknesses in the feminist response to what she saw as a crisis in contemporary life. It reflected the inadequacy of feminist understandings of childhood, heterosexuality and female subjectivity. In particular, it reflected a voluntarism which assumed that changes could be effected without psychic consequences. She noted that many feminists who had served as the shock troops of family change had become victims of what she called the 'failure of voluntarism'.

> Avoiding marriage and motherhood proved far easier, of course, than attaining gender equality, let alone liberation. The social, structural and cultural changes necessary for the latter remain far

from view . . . . Three sorts of personal traumas seem to be particularly widespread among those who shunned traditional marriage
and childrearing arrangements: "involuntary" singlehood, involuntary childlessness, and single parenthood.

(Stacey 1986: 239)

Stacey called for further feminist work on intimacy, child rearing,
childlessness and sexuality. She developed three themes. Firstly,
she argued that efforts to reconcile egalitarian relationships with
long-term commitment placed considerable strains on relationships. Secondly, she argued that there was a need for feminist
theories of child development which did not neglect the question
of what children need. This gap in existing feminist theory had been
filled, she argued, by the conservatives. Thirdly, she argued that
feminist theory was vulnerable in its treatment of heterosexuality
and this related to deeper problems in feminist theory and politics.
In particular, the notion of 'false consciousness' functioned to
assume that heterosexuals were dopes and fostered arrogance
on the part of feminist theorists. Paralleling Snitow's question
about what is required from men, Stacey asked: What are we looking for?

Is it woman or gender justice? Most . . . seem to presume that it is
the former or that the two are indistinguishable. Thus many
feminists have adopted a woman-identified stance as the best
strategy toward the goal of equality between women and men.
But for a good many feminists, woman identification has become
an end-in-itself and one that can lead . . . to a retreat from politics
or that can evolve into a simple affirmation of femaleness that
turns readily into a variation on Elshtain's "social feminism". The
latter approach tends to ignore, or even to thwart, the goal of
gender justice.

(Stacey 1986: 242)

This passage seems prescient in the light of the strong criticism by
writers such as Roiphe (1993) and Wolf (1993) against a feminism
that has posed male sexuality as automatically aggressive and has
seemed to have no positive vision of heterosexuality. (In the British
context, see the debates in *Feminism and Psychology*, starting with
the special issue on heterosexuality published in 1992.) Furthermore, implicit in the failure to countenance a positive role for
heterosexuality was a failure to posit a positive role for men. This

has had implications for men's involvement with children. Whilst Stacey's points are extremely important and I agree with them, the further feminist work she calls for cannot usefully be accomplished without using psychoanalysis, albeit critically.

In the UK, this kind of polarisation did not occur, although Coward (1993) noted the increasingly common phenomenon of high-profile women using motherhood to repudiate feminism and to demonstrate that feminism was wrong about what women really wanted. Only in the 1990s have debates on mothering, feminism and the family begun to take shape. These have focused on lone mothering and feminists have played a largely reactive role in them. The reasons for this include their marginalisation in the media, divisions about the role of men, the dominance of theoretical approaches which have been overly socially determinist and therefore unable to address questions about the impact of change at a psychological level, and antipathy towards considering children's needs.

FEMINISM AND MOTHERING IN THE UK IN THE 1990s

British feminist work on mothering is marked by a pervasive dualism in which the individual and the society are juxtaposed in mutually exclusive (and mutually suspected) explanations. Explanations in terms of social forces have been privileged and there has not been a thoroughgoing critique of the ensuing social determinism (see Hollway 1995). There is a tendency to assume that the structures, institutions and practices of mothering have clear-cut and uniform effects (see, for example, Richardson 1993). What is lost in the process are accounts of maternal subjectivity which can take into account the ways that fantasy, meaning, biography and relational dynamics inform individual women's positions in relation to a variety of discourses concerning motherhood.

Furthermore, motherhood is often posed as an initial event, despite Gordon's (1986) warnings, and there is often little attention given to the everyday practices that mothers carry out on behalf of, and with, their children. Writers such as Ribbens (1994) do explore everyday practices of child rearing but their stress on how children's needs have been constructed out of professional/expert agenda or prescriptions, which have been largely developed by white, middle-class men, can lead to an exclusive emphasis on freeing women and mothers from these normative impositions. Ribbens's call to refrain from judgement and evaluation side-steps complex dilemmas about the tension between women's and children's needs, interests and rights. It also ignores questions about whether any standards of evaluation are needed and, if so, what these might be. In so doing, it leaves health visitors and social workers unsupported in the face of, for example, maternal neglect and abuse (see Featherstone, Chapter 11). It also leaves feminist writers on the sidelines in popular discussions of what children need.

In the UK, there has not therefore been much progress by feminists in responding to Stacey's question about what it is children need. Indeed, there is either an antipathy to the question or it becomes focused on how anti-sexist child rearing should operate (see, for example, Richardson 1993). The debates on lone mothering have been the place where anxieties concerning men, women and children have recently been played out, using the currency of rights, responsibilities and needs.

LONE MOTHERING

Lone mothers have increasingly become seen in the UK and the USA not only as problems in themselves but as the source of other problems. Blaming single mothers for the rise in juvenile crime in the UK goes back as far as 1974, but recent attacks have been comparatively vitriolic (Mann and Roseneil 1994). The concern appears to be about the damage lone mothering does to boys and men: boys are no longer being provided with good role models and adult men are being deprived of the civilising influence that marriage brings. Alongside the confusion about whether the women involved are selfish, feckless or reflecting a new confidence and assertiveness are similarly confused messages about men and fathers. Are they, as influential commentators such as Murray (1990) and Halsey (1992) appear to suggest, essentially barbarians for whom marriage is a civilising force, or are they, as Lasch (1977) suggested, a vital source of moral authority for growing boys. When 2-year-old James Bulger was murdered by two 10-year-old boys in February 1993, concern about rising juvenile crime in Britain rose to a crescendo of moral panic about the kinds of family that could produce children capable of such a horrendous act. In particular, links were made with the rising rate of divorce and the growth in numbers of lone mothers.

Because the debates on lone mothers have often been offensively anti-women and anti-poor, they have been dismissed by feminists as evidence of moral panic or as further evidence of women being blamed for men's fecklessness. Furthermore, the exclusive focus on children's needs in these debates seems like yet more evidence that women are only seen as servicers of children and not as individuals with needs of their own.

However, these debates do raise important questions, notably: How do we manage and mediate between the needs, rights, responsibilities and expectations of family members in changing times? What kinds of help and support are required to cope with emotional, material and psychic distress? This distress is not new but is expressed differently under differing social arrangements. The distress engendered in nuclear families is conveniently forgotten in the focus on lone mothers (Samuels 1995), but it is not helpful to deny that divorce, separation and lack of stability in alternative childcare arrangements may also involve considerable distress; they clearly do. Susie Orbach (Chapter 6) suggests that divorce can be managed in such a way as to ameliorate the damage and hurt of separation, and she has been involved in formulating proposals on mediation to be included in government legislation. Such proposals have to be clear on what should be expected of men. Snitow (1992) argues that feminists have failed to resolve what they want from men in relation to children and to family life. For Hester and Radford (1996), contemporary developments around contact and mediation are problematic because, in their view, they fail to take account of power imbalances between men and women and do not acknowledge the risks women and children face from men in terms of violence and abuse. Focusing disproportionately on issues of violence and abuse without considering the need for children to retain contact with fathers is, in my view, an example of a regrettable tendency among feminists to highlight only the oppressive aspects of men's behaviour.

A related issue concerns how children deal with their parents forming new sexual and emotional attachments (see Hollway, Chapter 4); a situation with which a great number of women are coping on an everyday basis. What kinds of support are required? How can all concerned be helped to deal with the jealousies, anxieties and rivalries which ensue? The feminist focus on the possibility of sexual abuse by stepfathers in such situations has been important in ensuring that this possibility is not suppressed or denied, but it has provided few insights into the complexities and dynamics involved. To suggest that all men are potential abusers of children is to foster a paranoid climate in which women are encouraged not to trust any men who could help them in child care.

The overarching question of children's attachment to parents and other family members may be at the heart of some of the current disagreements. Those using feminist psychoanalytic perspectives would all share the view that the quality of emotional care offered to children in their early years has consequences for later development. Some of the more sociologically inclined feminist work ducks this issue by exploring how such developmental theories have been used to oppress women and impose normative constraints on them.

FEMINISM, PSYCHOANALYSIS AND MOTHERING: KEY CONTEMPORARY THEMES

Psychoanalytic work on mothers and daughters (see Ernst, Chapter 5) has moved from an early emphasis on relatedness and connectedness to acknowledging negative feelings such as anger, violence and claustrophobia. Flax (1990) has drawn a distinction between theorists who are their 'mothers' good daughters', stressing love, connection and oneness, and those theorists who explore the range of emotional dynamics which may occur between mothers and daughters. Parker's work on maternal ambivalence (Chapter 2) is of central importance here in that it argues that creative thinking about caring for children is enabled by the ambivalent holding together of love and hate.

Most feminism, in common with other political positions on motherhood, has assumed a rational individual child whose needs are met by meeting the needs of its mother. In contrast, most psychoanalytic feminism is now informed by understanding how the young child's mind produces in fantasy a mother who is more powerful than in reality, even omnipotent (Dinnerstein 1976). The 'fantasy of the omnipotent mother' (Chasseguet-Smirgel 1976) may not be significantly modified by the imposition of reality as the infant develops: it lives on, to a greater or lesser extent, in the unconscious and informs relationships not just with a person's mother but with women in general and with cultural and political discourses on mothering. Chodorow and Contratto (1989) argue that such fantasies are evident in feminist writings on motherhood, too, reminding women that, although some of us are mothers, we are all daughters. More primitive (early infantile) defences, such as splitting, will often be called upon to defend against the anxieties provoked by such omnipotence, leading to the idealisation and denigration of mothers which is characteristic of political discourses. Feminist writers who avoid the complexity of mothering, who fail to hold on to their own ambivalence, will reproduce these splits and leave defensive omissions in theorising motherhood which can be readily filled by right-wing discourses.

Flax (1990) has demonstrated how processes of repression and displacement operate in feminist writings generally, leading to overly coherent and closed theories. Sayers (1995) has argued that such processes can operate in relation to fathers and men in general. This can be true of feminist psychoanalytic writings as well as more general feminist writings, and casts light on the feminist battle lines drawn, particularly in the USA, over 'victim' feminism's tendency to see men's power as monolithic (omnipotent).

Benjamin (1995a, 1995b) develops Fast's (1990) distinction between repudiation (defensive rejection) of the parent of the other sex and renunciation (realistic giving up) of the characteristics of the other sex (see Frosh, Chapter 3 and Hollway, Chapter 4). She stresses the unconscious elaboration of 'opposite-sex feelings/behavior/attitudes ... which comprehends both cross-sex identification and the ability to represent and symbolize the role of the other in sexual relations' (1995b: 69). The development of non-defensive and non-polarised gender identities also facilitates the capacity to relate more ambivalently to mothers and fathers, and to motherhood and fatherhood.

Finally, the recent focus on maternal subjectivity in feminist psychoanalysis has the potential to transcend the dualistic conflict of 'either' children's 'or' mother's needs: 'Whereas history has recognized maternal work almost exclusively in terms of its impact on the child, contemporary culture is beginning to articulate the mother as a subject in her own right' (Bassin, Honey and Mahrer Kaplan 1994: 9). Through theorising the central importance of mutual recognition in mother–child relationships, Benjamin has argued that, in order to achieve an autonomous sense of self, a child needs a mother who is also autonomous. This is because a child cannot experience recognition by someone that he or she controls. Understanding children's developmental need for an autonomous maternal subjectivity is a far cry from early psychoanalytic tendencies (themselves probably overstated in feminist critiques) to posit a mother whose identity is entirely constituted through her child's demands. Benjamin's formulation does not magically reconcile the constant tensions between the mothers' own and their children's desires which mothers have to contain on an everyday basis, but it does point out the need to recognise the inevitable tension between autonomy and dependence: 'at the very moment of realizing our own independent will, we are dependent upon another to recognize it' (Benjamin 1995b: 37). In other words, we need to maintain the paradox between our earliest desires for a mother who is a need-satisfying other and our desires to be in control of our own lives. An emphasis on intersubjectivity also reminds us that our desires and pleasures are not separate from those of others, that helping to promote the pleasures and desires of children is part of the pleasure of mothering. Mothering is not all joy, but it is not all sorrow either. Let us hold on to both; let us not deny the ambivalence, either in practice or in theory.

THIS BOOK

This book brings together writers from therapeutic, academic and social work backgrounds who use psychoanalytic approaches in their attempts to understand and work with women, children and men on their relations in families of various kinds. For example, the images of selfish and dangerous single mothers fuelling media and public debates are explored by Ros Coward in Chapter 7 . Susie Orbach is concerned to apply psychoanalytic insights to the construction of better-informed social policy (Chapter 6). Sheila Ernst (Chapter 5) traces feminist psychoanalytic thinking on the mother–daughter relationship and, along with Orbach, explores current rethinking on children's capacities to relate and become separate and the gendered influences of parents. Psychoanalytic therapists work with transference and counter-transference dynamics (that is, where emotions and meanings belonging to earlier relations are transferred into the therapy and experienced by both client and therapist in their relationship). Since these transferences most often derive from mothers and fathers, therapists can learn from their counter-transference experiences much about how their clients, as children, experienced their parents and how these early experiences have affected their adult identities.

Rozsika Parker demonstrates in Chapter 2 how useful the notion of ambivalence is in understanding not only the complex emotions involved in mothering but also cultural fantasies and fears about mothers. She moves us away from comforting ideas of an essential harmony between women and children. Parker explores how the cultural splitting of mothers into idealised or denigrated objects not only suppresses maternal creativity and induces maternal guilt but leads to impoverished public debates about mothers, mothering and children. Brid Featherstone (Chapter 11) develops Parker's insights by applying them to statutory social work, an arena in which women social workers routinely meet other women in extremely painful circumstances, where fantasies of rescue and persecution abound. Like Parker, Stephen Frosh's use of ambivalence, this time in relation to fathering (Chapter 3), gives us the tools to move away from either/or positions which tend to pose fathers as wholly desirable or useless. Not only is this unhelpful, but it fuels potentially dangerous processes where men find little space to talk about their ambivalence. His careful tracing of psychoanalytic thinking on the father shows how psychoanalysis can be used to support beliefs about the desirability of highly differentiated roles for fathers and mothers. Frosh expands the possibilities beyond these traditional formulations of fathering as necessary prohibition or lack.

Wendy Hollway, in Chapter 4, addresses the topical area of the issues facing separating or divorcing mothers and their children and identifies some of the unconscious dynamics likely to occur, especially the difficulties involved in relations with a new partner. Drawing on the work of Benjamin and the Kleinians, she considers the usefulness of Oedipal theories in understanding the threesome when it includes a sexual partner who is not the original parent.

In Chapter 8 Paddy Maynes and Joanna Best explore how psychoanalytic understandings can be used to develop therapeutic practices with women who have suffered not only extreme social and economic disadvantages but psychic and often sexual abuse and who, in therapy, are struggling to transform their own mothering practices in order to break what might otherwise become a cycle of abuse. This chapter is a timely reminder of the devastation that injustice and abuse wreak at the psychic level, as well as testimony to the transformative powers that we all carry. Sheila Ernst uses case examples from women-only and mixed groups in Chapter 10 to show how gendered dynamics in groups, including transference dynamics, reflect the formative relations in families and how group work can contribute in a unique way to helping women and men transform their gendered selves and relations. In Chapter 9,

Caroline Owens takes us into a child's world (in a way which, perhaps surprisingly, is rare in feminist writings) and illuminates a girl's struggle with anxieties about her attachment to and loss of her parents. The example also illustrates the fundamental psychic importance of both parents in a child's internal world.

In all, the chapters contribute to very important ongoing debates about mothering, fathering, needs, responsibilities and rights. In particular, they emphasise the necessity of attending to the dynamics which fuel such debates. If left unprocessed, our fears, fantasies and desires can block and paralyse us, but they can also be resources for progressive change if accorded thoughtful and careful attention.

ACKNOWLEDGEMENT

I am deeply indebted to Wendy Hollway for the very careful editing work carried out on this chapter, as well as the help and suggestions she has provided in relation to recent developments in feminist psychoanalytic thought.

REFERENCES

Bassin, D., Honey, M. and Mahrer Kaplan M. (1994) 'Introduction', in D. Bassin *et al.* (eds) *Representations of Motherhood*, London: Yale University Press.

Benjamin, J. (1995a) 'Sameness and Difference: toward an "over-inclusive" theory of gender development', in A. Elliott and S. Frosh (eds) *Psychoanalysis in Contexts: Paths between Theory and Modern Culture*, London: Routledge.

—— (1995b) *Like Subjects, Love Objects: Essays on Recognition and Sexual Difference*, Harvard: Harvard University Press.

Chasseguet-Smirgel, J. (1976) 'Freud and Female Sexuality', *International Journal of Psychoanalysis*, 57: 275–86.

Chodorow, N. (1978) *The Reproduction of Mothering*, London: University of California Press.

Chodorow, N. with Contratto, S. (1989) 'The Fantasy of the Perfect Mother', in N. Chodorow, *Feminism and Psychoanalytic Theory*, New Haven and London: Yale University Press.

Coward, R. (1993) *Our Treacherous Hearts: Why Women Let Men Get their Way*, London: Faber & Faber.

Dinnerstein, D. (1976) *The Rocking of the Cradle and the Ruling of the World*, London: Souvenir Press.

Elshtain, J. Bethke (1981) *Public Man, Private Woman*, Oxford: Martin Robertson.

Ernst, S. and Maguire, M. (1987) (eds) *Living with the Sphinx*, London: Virago.

Everingham, C. (1994) *Motherhood and Modernity: An Investigation into the Rational Dimension of Mothering*, Milton Keynes: Open University Press.

Fast, I. (1990) 'Aspects of Early Gender Development: Towards a Reformulation', *Psychoanalytic Psychology*, 6 (supplement): 105–17.

Feminism and Psychology (1992) Special issue on hetererosexuality, 2(3).

Firestone, S. (1970) *The Dialectic of Sex: The Case for Feminist Revolution*, New York: William Morrow.

Flax, J. (1978) 'The Conflict between Nurturance and Autonomy in Mother–Daughter Relationships and within Feminism', *Feminist Studies*, 2: 171–89.

—— (1990) *Thinking Fragments: Psychoanalysis, Feminism and Postmodernism in the Contemporary West*, Oxford: University of California Press.

Freely, M. (1995) *What about Us? An Open Letter to the Mothers Feminism Forgot*, London: Bloomsbury.

Friedan, B. (1963) *The Feminine Mystique*, Harmondsworth: Penguin.

Gordon, L. (1986) 'Feminism and Social Control: The Case of Child Abuse and Neglect', in J. Mitchell and A. Oakley (eds) *What Is Feminism?* Oxford: Basil Blackwell.

Halsey, A. H. (1992) 'Foreword' to N. Dennis and G. Erdos *Families without Fatherhood*, London: IEA Health and Welfare Unit, Choice in Welfare No. 12.

Hester, M. and Radford, L. (1996) 'Contradictions and Compromises: The Impact of the Children Act on Women and Children's Safety', in M. Hester, L. Kelly and J. Radford (eds) *Women, Violence and Male Power*, Buckingham: Open University Press.

Hollway, W. (1995) 'A Second Bite at the Heterosexual Cherry', *Feminism and Psychology*, 5(1): 126–30.

hooks, b. (1984) *From the Margin to the Centre*, Boston, Mass.: South End Press.

Lasch, C. (1977) *Haven in a Heartless World: The Family Besieged*, New York: Basic Books.

Lazarre, J. (1976) *The Mother Knot*, New York: Dell.

Mann, K. and Roseneil, S. (1994) 'Some Mothers Do 'ave 'em': Backlash and the Gender Politics of the Underclass Debate', paper presented to the 'Good Enough Mothering? Feminist Perspectives on Lone Motherhood' conference, University of Leeds, 6 May 1994.

Murray, C. (1990) *The Emerging British Underclass*, London: IEA Health and Welfare Unit.

Oakley, A. (1974) *The Sociology of Housework*, London: Martin Robertson.

Ribbens, J. (1994) *Mothers and their Children: A Feminist Sociology of Childrearing*, London: Sage.

Rich, A. (1976) *Of Woman Born: Motherhood as Experience and Institution*, New York: W.W. Norton.

Richardson, D. (1993) *Women, Motherhood and Childrearing* London: Macmillan.

Roiphe, K. (1993) *The Morning After: Sex, Fear and Feminism*, Boston, Mass.: Little Brown.

Ruddick, S. (1980) 'Maternal Thinking', *Feminist Studies*, 6 (2) Summer: 342–67.

—— (1989) *Maternal Thinking: Towards a Politics of Peace*, Boston, Mass.: Beacon Press.

Samuels, A. (1995) 'The Good-enough Father of Whatever Sex', *Feminism and Psychology*, 5(4): 511–30.

Sayers, J. (1995) 'Consuming Male Fantasy: Feminist Psychoanalysis Retold', in A. Elliot and S. Frosh (eds) *Psychoanalysis in Contexts: Paths between Theory and Culture*, London: Routledge.

Segal, L. (1995) 'Feminism and the Family', in C. Burck and B. Speed (eds) *Gender, Power and Relationships*, London: Routledge.

Snitow, A. (1992) 'Feminism and Motherhood: An American Reading', *Feminist Review*, 40, Spring: 32–51.

Stacey, J. (1986) 'Are Feminists Afraid to Leave Home? The Challenge of Conservative Pro-Family Feminism', in J. Mitchell and A. Oakley (eds) *What is Feminism?* Oxford: Basil Blackwell.

Wolf, N. (1993) *Fire with Fire*, London: Chatto & Windus.

Chapter 2

The production and purposes of maternal ambivalence

Rozsika Parker

Maternal ambivalence is curiously hard to believe in. Even while writing a book on the subject I often found myself doubting its very existence (Parker 1995). Was it simply an apocryphal excuse for mothers who hate their children? Was I offering empty reassurance by arguing for the hidden contribution to creative mothering that ambivalence can provide?

None of us find it easy to truly accept that we both love and hate our children. For maternal ambivalence constitutes not an anodyne condition of mixed feelings, but a complex and contradictory state of mind, shared variously by all mothers, in which loving and hating feelings for children exist side by side. However, much of the ubiquitous guilt mothers endure stems from difficulties in weathering the painful feelings evoked by experiencing maternal ambivalence in a culture that shies away from the very existence of something it has helped to produce.

Only in the context of humour can it be safely acknowledged. In novels, women's magazines and national newspapers, column after column is devoted to comic accounts of maternal ambivalence. Safely cloaking their 'confessions' in laughter, mothers admit to being forever enraged, entranced, embattled, wounded and delighted by their children.

The concept of maternal ambivalence is well established within psychoanalytic theory. But the way it is thought about betrays cultural assumptions in relation to motherhood which render ambivalence a source of shame or object of disbelief. Although most psychoanalytic writers view the capacity to experience love and hate towards the mother as a positive achievement for the developing infant, ambivalent feelings towards her baby are more often than not considered to be a problem for a mother.

To disclose the range of reasons why maternal ambivalence has tended to be regarded as pathological, we need to explore its treatment within the interrelated fields of psychoanalysis, cultural representations of motherhood and the social management of mothering. For the purpose of this chapter I shall focus on psychoanalytic theory. Some feminists have argued that psychoanalytic theory is so steeped in mother-blaming as to be unuseable. I want to suggest that psychoanalysis is necessary for any deep understanding of ambivalence but – and it is an important but – we have to reframe, realign and rewrite theory to illuminate this theme from a maternal perspective. I shall attempt to demonstrate how we can continue to employ conventional psychoanalytic theory, re-reading it thoroughly from a mother's point of view.

Of course, developmental psychology observes mothers in minute detail, but this is usually in their role as origin and environment in a theory of childhood worked out from the child's point of view. Life is looked at from the position of a child to the detriment of our understanding of adult maternal development. The extent to which any mother moves through developmental sequences, potentially generalisable yet unique and internal to her, tends to be ignored. Instead, mother and child are presented as misleadingly isomorphic when, in fact, there are differing psychosocial processes specific to each of them, as well as the mutuality and interaction on which psychoanalysis has focused. A mother experiences processes of separation, union and reciprocity just as the child does – but the psychological meanings of these moments are particular to her (Flax 1990).

Take for example a mother's response to an ill child aged 7. Suddenly, from having been the mother of a school-age child she becomes again the mother of a child who cries if she leaves the room. Some mothers return happily to being a life-support system. They feel confident of their capacity to provide the sort of care needed by a sick child – indeed, some prefer the kind of mothering demanded in this situation. Others feel pulled back to a state they had found fearful and claustrophobic. Their present stage of mothering takes for granted the child's mobility and viability, while the sick, regressed child suggests a frailty and demands a quality of attention they had moved beyond, perhaps with a sigh of relief.

In my work on maternal ambivalence, I do not suggest that there is a normal, fixed, correct line of maternal development. As in everything to do with mothering, maternal development is determined by individual experience. I simply want to signal that, rather than maternity being the culmination or destination of female development, having a baby is a step in an unending series of transformations for women.

Psychoanalytic preoccupation with infantile development has indeed obscured maternal development. But the problem is even more complex. The traditional focus of analytic understanding has meant that maternal ambivalence, and the associated desire to make reparation to the baby, have been considered primarily as an action replay in the mother of her infantile experiences of ambivalence towards her own mother. How she became (or failed to become) an ambivalent baby delimits how she becomes (or fails to become) a mother who can manage the vicissitudes of her adult experience of maternal ambivalence. In my view, this overlooks the specificity of maternal ambivalence and the ways it may be different from infantile ambivalence. The particular fears, desires and passions of motherhood – for example, the intense adult wish to protect a powerless baby – inflect a woman's experience of ambivalence in particular ways. As I shall argue, maternal ambivalence is determined by complex interactions of external and internal reality and has to be socially and culturally located. Hence, we cannot simply apply theories of infantile ambivalence to maternal experience. We need to explore the differences (as well as any possible similarities) between infantile and adult modes of ambivalence.

MANAGEABLE AND UNMANAGEABLE AMBIVALENCE

If we can re-read them from a maternal perspective, Melanie Klein and Donald Winnicott are the two psychoanalytic theorists who have most to offer in terms of understanding maternal ambivalence. A schematic summary of the ideas Klein first introduced in her paper 'A Contribution to the Psychogenesis of Manic-Depressive States' (Klein 1935) would run as follows: in the second quarter of the child's first year it begins to experience the mother as a whole person in contrast to the previous state in which the mother is phantasised as split into part objects, specifically into a persecuting and an ideal maternal image. Such splitting is due to the infant's inability to acknowledge that the parent it loves for gratifying it is the same entity as the parent it hates for frustrating it. According to Klein, with growing integration, the infant begins to experience the mother differently – now as a whole object who can safely be loved as a whole person. This second mode she terms the 'depressive position' because it is the essence of depression to have anxious feelings about damaging someone or something you love. It involves the gradual recognition that the loved and hated mother are one and the same. The quality of anxiety associated with the first, paranoid schizoid position and the depressive position is significantly different. With the former, anxiety is experienced on behalf of the self; in the latter, anxiety is felt for the other. For with the dawning of ambivalence, the mother is seen as a loved person who might potentially be lost and driven away by hatred. Though reparation can be attempted, harm is nevertheless felt to have been done. Therefore, with the depressive position comes a sense of responsibility, an awareness of there having been a relational history, a differentiation of self from others, and a capacity for symbol formation. But, equally associated with the achievement of the recognition of ambivalence are loss, sorrow and separation.

The importance of a mother negotiating her quite specific entry into a *maternal* depressive position is clear. Reversing Klein's schema, we shall see that it is the mother's achievement of ambivalence – the awareness of her coexisting love and hate for the baby – that can promote a sense of concern and responsibility towards, and differentiation of self from the baby. Accordingly, both idealisation and denigration of her baby diminish. Acknowledging that she hates where she loves is acutely painful for a mother and feels terribly dangerous, for her baby is dependent upon her. Hence the sense of loss and sorrow that accompanies maternal ambivalence cannot be avoided. The parallel is with the loss Klein's baby undergoes when it gives up the image of the all-perfect, all-loving mother.

Klein came to believe that ambivalence existed very early in life, 'being already experienced in relation to part objects' (Klein 1952: 166). This implies that, even in infancy, the quality of ambivalence is changeable. As the child develops, the nature of ambivalence changes with the increasing *rapprochement* of love and hate. Klein describes:

> the all-important process of bringing together more closely the various aspects of objects (external, internal, 'good' and 'bad', loved and hated), and thus for hatred to become actually mitigated by love – which means a decrease of ambivalence. While the separation of these contrasting *aspects* – felt in the unconscious as contrasting *objects* – operates strongly, feelings of love and

hatred are so much divorced from each other that love cannot mitigate hatred.

(Klein 1940: 349)

Klein's phrase 'a decrease in ambivalence' is somewhat confusing. From a developmental standpoint, her overall theory suggests that ambivalence is an achievement – the capacity to tolerate the coexistence of love and hate. Yet here she seems to be depicting ambivalence as increased or decreased. But, where maternal ambivalence is concerned, surely what increases or decreases are the levels of guilt and anxiety provoked by the coexistence of love and hate. Perhaps, in this case, Klein has conflated 'ambivalence' and 'anxiety'. To minimise such confusions I have avoided referring to ambivalence as increased or decreased; instead, I speak of manageable and unmanageable ambivalence to distinguish between the experience of ambivalence as a source of creative insight, and ambivalence which arouses intolerable levels of guilt. When manageable, the pain, conflict and confusion of the coexistence of love and hate actually motivate a mother to struggle to understand her own feelings and her child's behaviour. When unmanageable, the potential for ambivalence to foster thought and spark concern is overwhelmed by the anxiety generated when hate no longer feels safely 'mitigated' by love. One of a series of mothers I interviewed with maternal ambivalence in mind describes her feelings when in the grip of unmanageable ambivalence:

A mother is a provider. I felt mothers were supposed to satisfy, soothe and make children happy, contented and fat. I had a boy who refused food and who cried. It tormented me beyond endurance to feel useless, unlovable and unloving.

For this mother, ambivalence was rendered unmanageable by the snowballing interaction of cultural representations of good and bad mother with the particular emotional meanings motherhood maintained for her. Had she simply felt unloving, she would not have found the experience so painful. It was the unmanageable coexistence of love and hate that rendered her so intolerably conflicted and anxious.

ASPECTS OF ANXIETY

We can go on to think about mothers' anxiety in relation to ambivalence in terms of Klein's description of persecutory and depressive anxiety. Once again, the theory has to be rethought so as to make it applicable to adult maternal, as opposed to infantile, processes. Maternal persecutory anxiety involves a mother's phantasised experience of herself as punished and tormented by her infant – no matter the difference in power between them, no matter that such phantasies may mostly be due to her own projections. She can feel annihilated, devoured and devastated by a child's apparently wilful determination to humiliate her and frustrate her needs. Maternal depressive anxiety, on the other hand, relates to a mother's (usually) unrealistic worry that she will have damaged the baby by her destructive impulses towards her or him. Turning again to the mother quoted above, it is clear that, in most mothers, persecutory and depressive responses to anxiety rarely exist in pure form. She needed her child to provide proof both that she was able to love and that she was loved. Instead, his distress sounded like an accusation and revelation of her capacity to hate and her hatefulness. She struggles not to attack her persecutor who she feels she is so badly letting down. The two kinds of maternal anxiety – depressive and persecutory – are intricately related. They coexist but their comparative strengths can fluctuate.

A patient of mine, whom I shall call Carla, illustrates how the nature of maternal anxiety can transform. A mother of three daughters and a son, she sought therapy with me because she felt she needed help in her relationship with her youngest daughter, then aged 13. All her life Carla had maintained a pattern of loving others 'despite' their behaviour towards her. She had anticipated motherhood as a state of unconditional, uncomplicated, unshadowed love. In this she is not alone. To a greater or lesser extent the hope that women carry into motherhood is that, at last, their love will be entirely welcome and put to good use. Carla told me, 'I have a need to love. It's inside me. I have had it all my life.' For years, she vigorously denied the element of hatred in her relationship with her daughter. Mia, her daughter, sensing the aspect of unreality in her mother's behaviour, persistently tried and tested her. In tears, Carla exclaimed to me, 'I never expected to have a child who would fight my love.'

Denying the complexity of her feelings for her daughter, she insisted that it wasn't that she hated Mia, it was simply that the girl was terribly persecuting. She was a Madonna of a mother to a Devil of a child, a sufferer from maternal persecutory anxiety. In other words, she felt 'done unto' by her daughter and could not bear to contemplate her own active aggressive phantasies in the situation.

Over the seven years of our work together, very slowly she became able to think about her profound unconscious guilt in relation to this child. Some years on, summing up her feelings as the split she had created between herself as all-loving and her daughter as all-hateful began to diminish, she said:

> I've been thinking about the word 'act' – to me it connotes perform. I've been either performing or reacting with Mia. Since I've been able to see the range of my feelings for her, I feel I've stopped performing the loving mother and I've stopped reacting with rage and hurt.

Carla realised that, rather than owning her love and hate for Mia, she had been self-righteously dancing to the tune of a maternal ideal. She would exclaim to me, 'I've loved that girl, I've given her everything.' But she withheld what she felt to be her authentic but utterly unacceptable feelings. She dated the change in their relationship, and in her mothering, from the moment when, during an argument she finally gave vent to her rage and exasperation, stuffing the drying-up cloth into her mouth and screaming.

Her new insights into her relationship with her daughter were accompanied by an increase in maternal depressive anxiety. Owning the complexity and conflictual nature of her feelings for Mia meant that she ceased to experience herself as the innocent victim of a persecuting daughter but began instead to question the assumptions she had brought to mothering. She responded to Mia's severe adolescent disruptiveness not with 'the problem is she's a bad girl' but with 'the problem is I'm a bad mother'. I hope it is clear how she swung between these two equally illusory modes of mothering.

She felt guilty, unhappy and helpless. Images of her own mother mocking her dominated her. The image of their own mother can often shape women's experience of mothering as a reproving presence or cautionary tale – making them feel they are either reproducing the mother they hated or letting down the mother they loved. Above all, as with Carla, their 'mother' – meaning the mother inside each of us – admonishes them for their ambivalence.

While Carla and I worked together, it became apparent that Mia herself was changing. She became significantly less antagonistic towards her parents. Perhaps she sensed a change in Carla, perceiving a greater authenticity in her mother's response to her, while simultaneously her own adolescent conflicts began to clarify. Slowly Carla herself became better able to think about her daughter and all the factors that had formed their relationship – not least the girl's relationship with her father. Turbulence still erupts between them. But Carla is no longer devastated by conflict and, instead of reacting defensively in crises, can struggle to think about what might be best for both her and her daughter.

This vignette draws upon many years' work, and I do not want to suggest that there is an ideal or optimal progression from persecutory anxiety to depressive anxiety in the experience of maternal ambivalence. The latter can be felt to be manageable or unmanageable, no matter what predominant form the anxiety generated. Depressive anxiety can produce incapacitating self-blame, while persecutory anxiety mobilises violent blame of the child. And, as I stated above, in mothers the two rarely exist in pure form.

A SOURCE OF INSIGHT

But what of manageable ambivalence? Melanie Klein's theory of reparation provides a partial answer as to why ambivalence in a mother can act as a spur to creative parenting. In 'Love, Guilt and Reparation' (Klein 1937) she elaborated her theory of ambivalence and related it to the experience of adult relationships, friendships, being a father and being a mother. She described how the urge to put right loved people who, in phantasy, have been harmed or destroyed becomes a crucial element in adult love. Because the conflict between love and hate is life-long, reparation plays a central part in the experience of being a parent. In Klein's view, maternal ambivalence signifies a re-experiencing of feelings a woman held in relation to her own mother during childhood. Thus, for example, the death wishes she harboured unconsciously towards her mother are now experienced in relation to her child, and are often complicated and magnified by associated conflictual feelings she had towards her brothers and sisters. And, just as she made reparation to her own mother for her destructive impulses, so she can make reparation to her children.

But Klein specifically situates maternal reparation as a form of *infantile* desire. The mother's intense relationship with her children mobilises her *infantile* wish to care and repair. The phenomenon of adult maternal hatred and its ramifications in the creative or destructive response it elicits in women is lost if we view it only from a reductive standpoint.

This becomes clearer if we consider that Klein's concept of reparation encompasses not only reparation of the object but also self-reparation. In other words, Klein's theory relates not only to making amends but to restitution. The pain engendered by the clash of love and hate for a child provokes the desire for self-reparation in a mother, with the restoration of the sense of maternal well-being which is fostered by love and shattered by the unacceptable face of hate. Arguably, however, where maternal ambivalence is concerned, reparation of the self and the object cannot be rigidly distinguished.

To regain her sense of well-being, a mother needs to abandon impossible maternal ideals which dangerously magnify both self-hate and child-hate. Bearing in mind the importance of maternal development, I have termed this process 'maternal individuation'. Here I am employing Jung's concept of individuation, which is defined as the development of the psychological individual as differentiated from the general or collective psychology (Jung 1921: 448–50; Samuels, Shorter and Plaut 1986: 76–9). Maternal individuation is an ongoing process in which ambivalence, coupled with the wish to experience the well-being of mother-love, pushes a mother into discovering ways of mothering which are congruent with her particular capacities and desires, rather than measuring herself against maternal mythologies.

I emphasise that this is a life-long process because adult ambivalence is not a static state of affairs but a dynamic experience of conflict, with fluctuations felt by a mother sometimes almost moment by moment, at different times in a child's development and varying between different children.

For example, at a certain period in her life, a woman with two children may experience acute conflict in relation to one of her children, with powerful hate only just balanced by passionate love, while harbouring easier feelings for the other child. There are many reasons for the discrepancy in a mother's response to individual children. She may have projected repudiated aspects of herself into the more hated child. Projection provides a benign means of unconscious to unconscious communication between mother and child. But projection can take a more malign form, in which unwanted or contradictory parts of the self are expelled and projected into other people who are then allocated various roles in the person's internal drama. If a mother unconsciously projects repudiated aspects of herself, she perceives them in her child and may hate what she sees. Of course, sometimes a mother learns about herself through observing her child. 'I can't bear his nervous watchfulness,' a mother said to me about her son, but added with sudden insight, 'I suppose it's too close to home!'

The theories of W. R. Bion are helpful in grasping the relationship between maternal ambivalence and maternal thinking (Bion 1962). But, once again, we cannot simply use the theory as it stands. For Bion employed the mother–child relationship as a model for the thought processes generated between psychoanalyst and patient. If we are to use his understanding of mothers, we have to move outside the consulting room to re-read his schema of maternal reverie with the power and inevitability of mother-love and mother-hate in mind.

Briefly, Bion's notion of reverie conceptualises a process that takes place between mother and child in early infancy. The baby projects unbearable feelings into the mother. A 'well-balanced' mother 'detoxifies' these feelings, makes sense of them for the baby in her mind, enabling the baby to feel understood and, in turn, to develop her or his capacity to understand.

For Bion, viewing the mother–baby interaction as a theoretical system intended for the use of practising analysts, the mother in unknowing knowingness is essentially a 'receptor organ' (Bion 1962: 116) and the goal is to remain balanced *vis-à-vis* the storming baby. Initially, this appears to be both an idealising and reactive model of mothering. The mother responds, reacts and replies to the messages directed to her via projective identification. When my children were babies I remember thinking ruefully how inappropriate the word 'reverie' seemed to be for my feelings in the face of my child's screams. Bion's good mother remains awe-inspiringly 'balanced' in the face of her storming baby. But I want to suggest that the term 'reverie', despite its passive associations, implies an active, albeit unconscious, capacity on the part of the mother to be in touch with her own turbulence.

Taking in a baby's projections can elicit a variety of painful responses: terror, anxiety, anger and concern. Hence a mother's understanding needs to be directed not only towards the baby but also to her own feelings. Unless she can begin to acknowledge her internal reality – which means facing the part of her that wants to shut the baby up at any cost, as well as the part that passionately wants to make things better – her capacity to help is limited. She needs to 'reverie' about herself if she is to understand her baby.

Bion describes the link between the containing mind and the contents put into it as manifesting three potentialities, 'L', 'H' and 'K', representing loving, hating and wanting knowledge about the content. The mother will consciously or unconsciously at times find herself loving, hating or trying to understand what her child is experiencing, thinking or feeling. To the conflict between love and hate, Bion added the conflict between knowledge ('K') or the desire to understand, and the aversion to knowing and understanding ('−K'). I am suggesting that, for a mother, the conflict between love and hate urgently mobilises 'K', the desire for knowledge. A mother's 'reverie' is a state of mind achieved by knowing the pain of conflictual feelings.

CREATIVE AGGRESSION

D. W. Winnicott also addressed maternal ambivalence but, like Bion's representation of the mother, Winnicott's mother is somehow shorn of turbulent affect. I think this is because, while he acknowledged the significance of maternal ambivalence for the emotional growth of the child, Winnicott's work contains relatively few references to the production and purposes of maternal ambivalence from the point of view of the mother (see Parker 1994). As a consequence of her or his own analysis, Winnicott claims, the analyst is able to tolerate hatred without retaliating. He expresses amazement that mothers (who have not had analysis) can tolerate hating their babies without retaliating. 'The most remarkable thing about a mother is her ability to wait for rewards that may or may not come at a later date' (Winnicott 1947: 202).

Winnicott's mother either responds by failing altogether to become conscious of hatred and simply falling back on masochism, or she sublimates her hatred by, for example, singing sadistic nursery rhymes 'which her baby enjoys but fortunately does not understand'. What Winnicott overlooks here is the creative role of hatred in maternal development. The singing of lullabies illustrates not only a way of safely containing hatred, but also how the painful coexistence of love and hate continually pushes a mother into the creative seeking out of reparatory solutions. In the depth of the night a baby's crying may prompt a mother to fantasise throwing her or him out of the window. At such times a mother's love may be overwhelmed by persecutory anxiety, promoting the impulse to attack the persecuting baby, and stymying the reparatory process. In other words, ambivalence may be unmanageable. But, equally often, the painful conflict between love and hate can in itself provoke and strengthen the mother's desire to know and answer the baby's needs. Instead of acting upon the violent impulse, mothers may create solutions such as singing lullabies, rocking or feeding.

Winnicott wanted mothers to be conscious of ambivalence for the sake of the children. He wrote that 'children seem able to deal with being hated', and 'they can meet and make use of the ambivalence which mother feels and shows'. But what they cannot use in their emotional development 'is mother's repressed unconscious hatred which they only meet in their living experiences in the form of reaction formation'. Winnicott explained, 'At the moment the mother hates she shows special tenderness. There is no way a child can deal with this phenomenon' (Winnicott 1969: 250).

Winnicott's insistence that a child both needs and utilises the experience of being hated is important, but the distinction he draws here between conscious and unconscious hatred raises real problems. It demands a degree of consciousness that denies how deeply rooted hate is in the unconscious. And it requires a degree of control over hatred that would inevitably negate the intense conflict between love and hate that characterises ambivalence. I think we need to dispense with Winnicott's division of hatred into 'good' conscious hatred and 'bad' unconscious hatred, and rather to think in terms of different expressions of hatred. Hatred without love – hatred without ambivalence – can be entirely destructive and can lead to gross abuse. And hatred accompanied by terrible shame and fear fostered by a culture which cannot bear to contemplate maternal ambivalence can also lead to the kind of reaction formation Winnicott describes. Nevertheless, although it may be hard to accept, it is the unruly, unacceptable nature of hatred that itself can breed thought and concern; aggressive fantasies, violent impulses in concert with loving feelings, can bring women face to face with themselves and with their children (Samuels 1989). Some can bear it; some can use it in their maternal development; some find it unbearable.

Winnicott's concept of the 'stage of concern' (Winnicott 1950/ 1955) can be deployed to clarify that there is indeed beneficial aggression contained within maternal ambivalence. Although his primary focus is on the child's experience, we can reframe his description of the transformation of aggression into social functions to illuminate maternal processes. He coined the term 'stage of concern' for the developmental moment when aggression is transformed and appears as grief or guilt. In common with many other object relations theorists, Winnicott salutes as a major milestone the attainment of a capacity by an infant to sustain and manage depression. It involves a sufficient degree of personal integration to accept responsibility for the destruction that is part of life. But we do not find much in Winnicott about depression in mothers as an achievement. Concern for the negative impact of clinical maternal depression on the developing child marries up with cultural representations of the unalloyed joy of motherhood to outlaw the degree of depression or creative grief that is a necessary and beneficial product of ambivalence. It feels almost sacrilegious to suggest that mothers need to be depressed.

However, if a mother can hold on to the depression, aggression and grief mobilised by ambivalence, it can be beneficial in a number of ways. Winnicott writes that, 'a normal, healthy mother is able to summon up ambivalence in object-relating and to be able to use it appropriately'. The context of this comment was a discussion of a mother who experienced problems around weaning and complained that her child 'will not wean' when, in Winnicott's view, the mother 'may well be in a depressive phase in which hate (both active and passive) is not available to consciousness for use in relationships' (Winnicott 1965: 146). In my rather different terms, excessive depressive anxiety provoked by the coexistence of love and hate has rendered ambivalence unmanageable and the mother paralysed; whereas, with manageable ambivalence, the degree of depression evoked by the coexistence of love and hate for a child mobilises a mother's concern and capacity to think.

Winnicott's reference to the constructive potential of hatred is frustratingly elusive, but we can pursue the implications of his comment by taking his description of a specific moment in infantile development, which he terms 'use of an object' (Winnicott 1971). Again I will re-read this from the mother's point of view.

Winnicott contrasts object relating with what he calls 'the use of an object'. The former implies that the other is a composite bundle of the subject's projections that can be controlled in the mind. By contrast, in object usage the other functions as an entity the infant can use, one that may inhabit a shared reality but is not nearly so susceptible to manipulation or control. The process by which a subject places an object outside her or his control involves the destruction of the object. Paradoxically, destruction of the object implies it is located outside the self, meaning outside the self's control. The baby's sense of separateness is thus enhanced. The role of the mother is to survive the destruction, not to retaliate, and hence prove to the baby that loving separation is indeed possible.

I want to suggest that a parallel but different process to the infant's is going on in the mother: a 'maternal use of infant-as-object'. Now it is the mother who has to cease experiencing the infant as part of herself and begin to acknowledge its separate reality. For the mother to do this, she has to go through a process of 'destroying' the infant-as-object. Here it is her ordinary phantasies of destroying her baby that are paradoxically helpful to the separation process. Only when she 'destroys' infant-as-object can she be said to have placed the baby outside her area of omnipotent control. Only via 'destroying' her baby can she be said to have achieved the full 'use of an infant', meaning the achievement of a relationship to the baby as a person separate from herself. For this process to remain benign and for the baby to survive, the mother's hate-inspired process to 'infant usage' needs to be accompanied by recognition of her ambivalence – hate being vital for destruction and love for keeping this on a psychic and not a physical level.

A mother of two older children, faced with her first major separation from them, exemplifies the difficult but potentially creative coexistence of aggression and protection, love and hate, in the process of separation. Mary's children, aged 6 and 9, were invited to go to Norway for ten days with a friend's family. She said to me:

> I long for them to go. I can't wait to see the back of them. When was the last time I had ten days all to myself. But I also feel terrible about it. I'm scared of losing them. I have images of planes crashing, drowning and abduction, and I want to say that they can't go. It's terrible to want to get rid of them and to want so much to hold onto them.

On the one hand, her aggression evoked persecuting images of disaster that made separation feel dreadfully unsafe. Yet, on the other hand, her aggression enabled her to own the desire for time for herself. In other words, the sensation of rage and frustration both provoked her into an awareness of her needs and provided the energy to pursue them. Sometimes, anger and hate can be sources of a mother's sense of separateness and thus of her autonomy. Love for the child can contain the anger and hate, rendering it a constructive rather than destructive force for separation. In Mary's case, she had reached a point in her maternal development when she could see the children as independent rather than as extensions of herself. Though deeply conflicted, she could 'let them go' while at the same time instituting 'safety nets' – a reliable system of phone calls.

The recognition by a mother that she has her own needs and priorities is, as Jessica Benjamin amongst others has argued, crucial for a child's development. It is not enough for a mother simply to mirror her child's attainments and accomplishments, she has to offer the child the experience of engaging with another autonomous being if the child is to develop a sense of herself or himself as a person in her or his own right (Benjamin 1988).

At every stage, development involves baby or child in a conflict between self and other. A parallel state of affairs holds true for the mother. For her, the recognition of both her needs and her child's desires is a constant and necessary struggle in her development. And, as we can see from Mary's experience, the conflict is given an added poignancy because her needs are inextricably linked to her child's well-being. She wants to feel she is the good mother of a well and happy child. Ambivalence saves her from oversubmission on the one hand and excessive domination on the other.

I have been arguing that, because of the conflict it evokes, manageable ambivalence can quite literally make a woman think. It can be a force for concern and a focus for contemplation of her relationship with a child. I have also highlighted the potentially beneficial outcome of the aggression mobilised by the coexistence of love and hate. I want now to turn to what renders ambivalence unbearable – to unmanageable ambivalence.

POWER AND LOSS

Thinking about mothering demands our holding in mind many complex interactions of inner and external reality. A woman's personal, cultural and ethnic history, her economic circumstances, her relationships, the psychological and physical state of her child can all impact on her response to ambivalence. Central to what renders ambivalence unmanageable is every woman's desire to be a good mother in concert with the quite specific fears and anxiety mobilised by the state of late twentieth-century motherhood. A 1995

Barnardo's report, tellingly headlined in the *Guardian* as 'Children "under house arrest" ' (Wright 1995) was in fact a survey of mothers' attitudes towards their children's safety. It revealed mothers' lives to be dominated by fears of strangers, traffic and drugs.

Anxiety about loss in the context of feelings of both power and powerlessness are central to motherhood. We speak of 'getting pregnant' or 'having a baby', but also of 'losing a baby'. And, indeed, the atmosphere generated by antenatal medical care suggests that if a mother loses her baby it is through her own carelessness:

> I really enjoyed pregnancy up until the fifth month. It sounds corny but I felt 'fecund' – free at last to be fat, creative and full of myself. Then my blood pressure went up. I was ordered to be careful, to rest, to watch my weight gain, etc. From feeling at one with the baby, he became the opposition, the source of my failure who threatened me with pain.

From the moment of conception the social management of pregnancy and birth imposes a contradictory sense of omnipotence on a mother. She is in other people's hands, yet feels herself to be responsible for producing a healthy baby with a good birth experience. To herself, she is both huge and horribly small. She can experience a wonderful plenitude coexisting with terror of emptiness, loss and fear of failure. Psychologically speaking, each step of a child's development could be thought of as a loss.

The experience of unmanageable ambivalence is intricately linked to anxieties around loss. The fear that dominates infantile ambivalence is the fear that hatred will damage and drive away the loved mother. Similarly, mothers have to contend with the fear that loss of the child will be incurred through hating the child. In other words, that her hatred will cost her the child's love. And, crucially, mothers experience the fear of loss evoked by ambivalence in the context of the cultural expectations of maternal power, social curtailment of that power, her own desire for potency, her conviction of powerlessness, and her loving concern for her child.

Freud and Klein discussed the manner in which, during adult life, the ultimate loss – bereavement – intensifies the conflict between love and hate. I am suggesting that motherhood constantly brings about something akin to the states of mind Klein considered to be evoked by mourning (Klein 1940). I shall first describe Klein's depiction of what is involved in the experience of loss and then relate it to maternal experience. She considered loss to be especially significant because of its impact upon the internal good-object which is synthesised out of an absorption of experiences with real others and unconscious phantasy structures:

> It produces a sense of there being a good, helpful figure inside the personality felt to reside there, and so closely loved as to constitute the basic primary identification around which the whole of an identity is formed. The good internal object provides the continual internal dialogue of encouragement and self-esteem on which confidence and psychological security are based.
>
> (Hinshelwood 1989: 142)

Loss, bereavement, rejection may threaten the phantasy of there being actually a good thing – a good internal object – inside oneself that nourishes other people. This induces guilt – guilt that harm has been done to a loved person. Too severe and punishing a sense of guilt evokes defensive evasions. Instead of guilt leading to remorse, mourning and reparation, it calls into play a failure to mourn, characterised by paranoid and manic defences. Denial, idealisation, splitting and control are all employed by the ego to counteract persecutory anxiety – and to a lesser extent depressive anxiety. Klein comments, 'When anxiety is paramount, the ego even denies that it loves the object at all' (Klein 1952: 73).

If we take a scene familiar in any playground, we can see how mothering institutes at telescopic speed the processes Klein describes in unresolved mourning, but with ambivalence often rendered unmanageable by the quite specific anxieties mobilised by motherhood. In defiance of its mother, a child climbs to the top of the tallest slide. As it swoops down to the foot of the slide the mother rushes forward and brutally slaps the child. How might we understand what is going on here? I would suggest that the defiant child has summoned up in its mother both the terrifying prospect of losing her child and a quite shocking loss of maternal identity. Thus, for the moment, the child has become her persecutor, and her love for the child and the culture's expectation of maternal behaviour combine to accuse her of inadequacy. She slaps because she hates the child for behaviour that threatens her with the loss of an internal object called 'me-as-a-good-mother', for turning her into a monster, and for obscuring the love and concern that are obviously also there.

The playground scenario highlights how, in most mothers, persecutory and depressive maternal anxieties are intricately linked. As the child swoops down the slide, the mother feels both that she is a bad mother and that the child is bad to have scared her so. A mother faced with real or imagined loss, who cannot trust her capacity to put things right, is a mother who, at least temporarily, when overwhelmed with anxiety, cannot manage ambivalence. Then she may resort to manic omnipotence and denial of her love for her child. Her dependence on her relationship with her children is denied and fears of their loss do not give rise to anguish and guilt.

Cultural expectations are partly responsible for the times when the anxiety associated with ambivalence becomes unbearable and anxiety on behalf of the child transforms into aggression against the child or the self. A mother of a 7-year-old girl describes the way her expectations of herself as a mother become conflated with what she feels is expected of her as a mother:

> In the car Kate won't sit in her booster seat. She insists on sitting on the arm rest and wearing the lap belt. I insist. She refuses. I know I have right on my side but I can't get her to do what I want. I get angrier and angrier. I start thinking, if we do crash, and she does break her pelvis, who is going to do all the work of looking after her – me! And who is going to get the blame – me!

One expectation facing mothers which is guaranteed to intensify the anxiety generated by the coexistence of love and hate is that they can, and indeed should, exercise an all-inclusive 'control' over themselves and their children. But psychoanalytic theories have revealed the power of the unconscious, emphasising how limited is our real control over children, even when we seem to be in control. A mother said to me,

> I don't want Sally and Keith to share my fears. I'm terrified of so many things – of dogs in particular. I really didn't want them to be scared of dogs. For their sake I tried to overcome my terror, even managing to take a neighbour's dog to the heath. But despite everything, Keith's got all my fear of them and Sally's sort of hesitant with them.

Unconscious to unconscious communication ensured that Carol's children felt her fear of dogs. Despite the power of unconscious processes, our society continues to have grandiose expectations of mothers. And mothers, with their profound desire to be good mothers, both reproduce and resist these expectations. Wanting to control the uncontrollable, a mother feels painfully culpable when things go wrong. Yet, even while mothers are accorded overwhelming responsibility for their children's development, their authority is all the time circumscribed, subjected as they are to the critical gaze of a network of social structures.

Women mother within cultures that maintain impossible, contradictory maternal ideals which render the range of feelings considered 'normal' or 'natural' in mothers narrow indeed. Hence maternal ambivalence is viewed askance and defended against by both idealisation and denigration of mothers. Ambivalence of itself is not automatically a problem. But the shame that often surrounds it renders it deeply problematic.

ACKNOWLEDGEMENTS

My thanks are due to my patients who have given me permission to write about their experience of being mothers, and to all those other mothers who, also remaining anonymous, agreed to be interviewed. I am grateful to Wendy Hollway and Andrew Samuels for perceptive criticism and constructive suggestions.

REFERENCES

Benjamin, J. (1988) *The Bonds of Love: Psychoanalysis, Feminism and the Problem of Domination*, London: Virago Press.

Bion, W. R. (1962) 'A Theory of Thinking', *Second Thoughts*, London: Maresfield Reprints, 1984.

Flax, J. (1990) *Thinking Fragments: Psychoanalysis, Feminism and Post Modernism in the Contemporary West*, Berkeley: University of California Press.

Hinshelwood, R. D. (1989) *A Dictionary of Kleinian Thought*, London: Free Association Books.

Jung, C.G. (1921) *Psychological Types. Vol. 5. Collected Works of C.G. Jung*, London: Routledge & Kegan Paul; Princeton, N.J.: Princeton University Press (1971).

Klein, M. (1935) 'A Contribution to the Psychogenesis of Manic-Depressive States', in M. Klein *Love, Guilt and Reparation and Other Works 1921–1945*, London: Hogarth, 1985.

—— (1937) 'Love, Guilt and Reparation', in *Love, Guilt and Reparation*.

—— (1940) 'Mourning and its Relation to Manic-Depressive States', in *Love, Guilt and Reparation*.

—— (1952) 'The Emotional Life of the Infant', in M. Klein *Envy and Gratitude and Other Works 1946–1963*, London: Hogarth, 1980.

Parker, R. (1994) 'Maternal Ambivalence', *Winnicott Studies*, no. 9.

—— (1995) *Torn in Two: The Experience of Maternal Ambivalence*, London: Virago Press. (Also as *Mother Love/Mother Hate: The Power of Maternal Ambivalence*, New York: Basic Books, 1996).

Samuels, A. (1989) *The Plural Psyche: Personality, Morality and the Father*, London and New York: Routledge.

Samuels, A., Shorter, B. and Plaut, A. (1986) *A Critical Dictionary of Jungian Analysis*, London and Boston: Routledge & Kegan Paul.

Winnicott, D. W. (1947) 'Hate in the Countertransference', in D. W. Winnicott *Through Paediatrics to Psycho-analysis*, London: Hogarth, 1982.

—— (1950/1955) 'Aggression in Relation to Emotional Development', in *Through Paediatrics to Psycho-analysis*.

—— (1965) 'The Concept of Trauma', in D. W. Winnicott *Psycho-Analytic Explorations: D. W. Winnicott* (eds C. Winnicott, R. Shepherd and M. Davis), London: Karnac, 1989.

—— (1969) 'Development of the Theme of the Mother's Unconscious as Discovered in Psycho-analytic Practice', *Psycho-Analytic Explorations: D. W. Winnicott*.

—— (1971) *Playing and Reality*, London: Tavistock.

Wright, N. (1995) 'Children Under House Arrest'. *The Guardian*, 22 August.

Chapter 3

Fathers' ambivalence (too)

Stephen Frosh

HAIL THE CONQUERING HERO

> The woman, Elizabeth, says to me: 'Look, my son needs a father, but he doesn't need *his* father.' Is this an invitation to enter into a vacant space? I am talking about therapy here, not marriage. Does she want me, a male therapist, to take over? Despite everything, despite all her experience of being everything to this child, she seems to believe that a boy needs a dad.

Psychoanalysis is a discipline of rationalism, of clear-headedness, and in the rationalist world view there is little doubt that fathering is preferred to mothering. Mothering is so *messy*, after all, so full of bodily functions. All that dripping and cleaning up, all that food on the floor, and much else besides, not to be confronted in the man's clean world. Children stop you thinking; everyone knows that they turn your brain to porridge.

Freud, in a work of his oldest age, expressed this beautifully in relation to his hypothesis that the supposedly historical transition from matriarchy to patriarchy was an 'advance for civilisation'.

> But this turning from the mother to the father points in addition to a victory of intellectuality over sensuality – that is, an advance in civilisation, since maternity is proved by the evidence of the senses while paternity is an hypothesis, based on an inference and a premise. Taking sides in this way with a thought process in preference to a sense perception has proved to be a momentous step.

(Freud 1939: 361)

Going out to work can be hard, goodness knows, but it has its benefits; amongst them the flight from mess, from the soft and spongy texture of dependence. Children can be thought about at a distance, symbols of achievement and continuity, but when they are needy, it is time to pass them over. Time for a rest. Parenthood as 'an inference and a premise' rather than the 'evidence of the senses': this sounds like the fathering many of us have known.

If psychoanalysis is thought of as a modernist project in which the intellect struggles to master the confusions of experience – including making sense of irrationality and unconscious emotion – then it is not surprising that the valued terms in a sequence of dichotomies line up as follows:

masculine–feminine
active–passive
intellect–emotion
rational–irrational
abstract–concrete
reality–fantasy
separation–dependence
paternal–maternal.

This is a sequence full of common sense rather than a specific psychoanalytic vocabulary, yet it is also emblematic of psychoanalytic orthodoxy in various forms. The great male progenitors of psychoanalysis, Freud above all, located fathering as something that rescues the child from the dangers of regressive absorption in the mother. Fathering is a limit placed on what can happen, an obstruction to and channelling of desire so that it is congruent with 'reality', that is, so that it takes forms which are socially acceptable and less liable to disruptiveness and subversion. In the classical psychoanalytic formulation, fathers become relevant to the child with the advent of the Oedipus complex, when the desire of the child becomes unbearably turned towards the mother, whether positively (the boy's sexual craving) or negatively (the girl's despondent repudiation). This desire is 'unbearable' in a specifically social sense: it cannot be borne by or in a social world structured around the prohibition on incest. For the child, the unbearable nature of direct desire is incorporated into the psyche; in Freud's formulation, it results in castration anxiety which in turn produces a new mental agency (the super-ego), internalising the external prohibition. More simply, the child comes to feel that too much intensity, too much closeness or antagonism, cannot be survived. What the father offers under these circumstances is distance, a breathing space that becomes a life-long separation. The boy is forbidden from taking his mother as a sexual partner, the girl is persuaded to return to her native state, hoping for the civilising influence of her own male baby at a later date. Everyone can rest easy, incest will not take place.

Although there are both attracting and repelling components to the father's function in relation to his children as theorised by classical psychoanalysis, the dominant imagery is one of prohibition. The mother *allows*, cossets and comforts, experiences her infant as part of herself, creates around him or her a translucent skin, a post-natal 'monad' in Béla Grunberger's (1989) scathing version of things. She pretends to the child that narcissistic absorption in the other is possible, that the demands of the world can be held at bay while mother and babe bathe in the light of Elysian fields. Then the father comes along, representative of reality, and says 'no' to all this: 'no' to the boy possessing the mother, 'no' to the girl having her own penis, 'no' to home. The child – or at least the male child – gets pointed outwards: here is reality; to this you have to succumb; prepare yourselves in this way for the worlds of war and work. The father's function is to make this incursion of reality viable, to set a boundary around the I–thou relationship so that everyone can see that it is allowed to exist only within the structures given to it by the outside.

For Grunberger, as for many other psychoanalysts, this function of the father is necessary for the mental health of the child and for the social polity. Without it, the individual collapses back into regressive narcissism, avoiding the world and searching for the illusory consolations of the womb. At its worst, such a collapse can result in a failure to tolerate difference of any kind, and consequently a relentless hunting for sameness – for the purity of the same as represented in fascist mythology. Grunberger makes it clear that such a psychological stance is built on a denial of Oedipal reality, and thus expresses an anti-paternal wish, a desire to obliterate the very possibility of fathering:

The Oedipal person reacts to failure as a stimulus to attempt the fulfilment of his Oedipal wishes with renewed determination, but for the narcissist there is no next time, since he prefers the disappearance of the system in which the injury took place ... He will not try to triumph over the father (to identify with him in order to surpass him later) but will try to abolish the principle of paternity itself and the whole frame of reference of which it was the organiser.

(Grunberger 1989: 39)

What is clear from this quotation is the sense in which the father has a role as he who frustrates the child – and hence makes it possible for the child to learn the value of limits and the necessity to strive to 'surpass' them. Without this frustration there is only wishing, living in the kind of world of narcissistic fantasy which produces endless disavowal of reality and lapses into self-aggrandisement and rage when faced with failure. The narcissist has no limit and hence has no sense of the boundaries of her or his self; this means that the self is both overinvested in, seen as all there is, and underresourced, experienced as having no stability, no anchoring or firm basis. With only absorption in the mother to fall back upon, the narcissist suffers from the fantasy that everything exists to serve her or his needs; as this is patently not the case, life becomes a series of painful punctures and regressive flights.

William says, 'He's a mummy's boy, always has been. She won't let him go, he's like a two-year-old. See him sitting on her lap, like a two-year-old. What does he want?' But it's his brother who throws stones. Is it, perhaps, the lack of care, the failure to allow regression and nurture, that has produced the delinquent? He certainly knows what paternal, Oedipal reality is; but he doesn't seem to like it, not one bit. Especially he doesn't like having to be 'same as' his father, while his brother, frightened of everything, finds comfort. Eventually, maybe, both will develop different kinds of armour; perhaps we won't be able to tell them apart.

Hail the conquering hero. The prohibitive influence of the father is also a productive one: by ending the child's absorption in the mother, it makes possible her or his engagement with difference, and therefore with reality. Limits placed upon the aggrandised self are not simply to be understood as restrictive, for by defining the boundaries of selfhood they also make possible an experience of boundedness, otherwise known as a consciousness of identity. There is now a possibility of something rooted: the paternal 'no' is a means of marking the desiring potential of the child as someone separate from the mother, hence capable of acting as well as of being stopped. In this reading, the father's word makes things happen, whereas before, as in Eden, they were static. Get out, no return, there is an angel with a flaming sword at the gate; the father, like the great Father, has said 'no' to what you (in fantasy) have done.

Lacan's gloss on this is even more penetrating. Making it all linguistic, Lacan emphasises the paternal 'no' in a literal way: the name ('nom') of the father is experienced as a no ('non'); speaking from his place as father, the father's voice is heard as one that breaks into the cosy illusions of narcissistic absorption and announces the creation of a cultural subject, the child as social being. At the developmental moment in which the father speaks, the infant is taken out of the register of the Imaginary (where a fantasy of wholeness predominates) and into the Symbolic, subject to all the demands and constraints of the linguistic and cultural order, but also capable of entering into transactions with others – of being a social self and of communicating as such. Eden may be lost, but at least human subjects can make something with their own hands – each one can make a name for him- or herself. And without this movement there is not only narcissism, but the risk of full-blown psychosis, creeping upon the individual who renounces the Symbolic, who 'forecloses' the word of the father.

> It is an accident in this register [of the signifier] and in what takes place in it, namely, the foreclosure of the Name-of-the-Father in the place of the Other, and in the failure of the paternal metaphor, that I designate the defect that gives psychosis its essential condition, and the structure that separates it from neurosis.
>
> (Lacan 1955/1956: 215)

Refusal of the 'paternal metaphor', of the Symbolic, means refusal of the social; there is no location of the individual subject in any meaningful array of symbols. The world swims away; the defining structures of subjectivity are renounced. Just as in classical psychoanalysis, Lacan's formulation makes the father's voice *necessary* for development and identity formation, necessary for sanity; not only must the father speak, but he must also be heard.

'Boys need a father and I am their father. You can see she can't manage them, so why do you side with her? You are an expert, you are a father too.' He appeals to me because he knows I too am a father, so I must also understand not just that fathers are necessary, but that mothers on their own are no good.

MOTHER-LOVE

The emphasis on the paternal voice to be found in classical and Lacanian psychoanalysis is not, of course, the only point of view in psychoanalytic theory as a whole. Object relations theory has dealt with the issue of prohibition by marginalising the father, making the mother the only real developmental force for the child while the father offers her support or a context in which her concentration on the child can continue undisturbed. The imagery of the father as offering a boundary or limit continues here, but with a character- istically less negative view: the father creates the setting allowing the work of mothering to take place, much as society needs to provide the setting in which the therapist and patient can work together undisturbed. (See Frosh (1987) for a discussion of the political implications of object relations theory.)

More interestingly, Kleinian psychoanalytic theory also margin- alises the father, or rather absorbs him in the mother, much as Kleinians suppose happens in the fantasy life of the child. Klein's theory is full of the mother's body: the child is enveloped in it, experiences it as the entire world, structures her or his own con- sciousness according to direct and phantasised experiences with it. The breast is more powerful than the penis; the infant's phantasy supposedly has the penis contained in (swallowed up by) the breast; and it is the breast as feeding object, as something with which there is a relationship unmediated by sight or language, which is the crucial performative force in the child's early experience. Moreover, throughout development it is the relationship with the breast that is constantly returned to, the breast being a symbol both of power (it is envy directed towards this, not penis envy, that is central to Kleinian thinking on destructiveness), and also of the extent to which the external world can be trusted to help the individual contain her or his own passion. Kleinian theory suggests that an experience of the breast as able to contain and 'feed back' the infant's early aggressive assaults without retribution, leads to an inner world resilient in the face of pressures towards splitting, and capable of deep feeling and integrated, reparative tendencies. This occurs because, whatever the state of internal chaos, there is in fantasy something 'out there' which has been and can continue to be loved.

The key dynamic concepts to be found in Kleinian thought are those of projection and introjection (along with projective and introjective identification), and envy (Segal 1973; Hinshelwood 1989; Frosh 1987). These are concepts based on metaphors of incorporation and expulsion which in turn are held to be founded on the actual experiences of the infant – the infantile world being dominated by immediate bodily sensations. The inner world is built up on the model not of the outer world but of sensations of feeding and excreting, and relatedly of being engulfed or abandoned. The outer world is then invested with these qualities through projection, commonly involving projection of pieces of the self into the other. So, distinctively, Kleinians produce a vision of the subject in continuous phantasised contact with the object, so much in contact that boundaries blur and it is possible to feel inside the self what is going on inside the other. The mother and infant are so mutually entangled that the experience of one is incorporated into the experience of the other; this is the prototype for all intense experiences throughout life.

Where is the father in all this? Eaten by the mother, it seems. Although Klein maintains a classical respect for the father in the Oedipus complex, the energy and verve of her theory lies unmistakably with its maternal components, and everything in it points to the domination of mother-psychology over father-psychology. It is not the father who allows the child to make contact with reality; rather, it is the capacity of the mother to manage the infant's envious projections that makes it possible for the child to become an integrated subject, capable of tolerating her or his internal destructiveness and distinguishing between inner and outer worlds. The infant certainly has to make a relationship with the father in this, but it takes place through the mother: just as 'reality' is only perceived and processed through a fog of phantasy, so the father is known initially through the internalised maternal object. Consequently, images of containment and holding in Kleinian thought as well as in object relations theory, do not take the form of a paternal limit but of a maternal capacity to remain stable and accepting in the face of aggressive intent. Hence, Bion's concept of *reverie*, the ideal analytic state of mind in which all projections can be held and tolerated, is rooted in maternal imagery, unlike the Freudian idea of the analyst as scientist-explorer.

> Reverie is that state of mind which is open to the reception of any 'objects' from the loved object and is therefore capable of the reception of the infant's projective identifications whether they are felt by the infant to be good or bad.
>
> (Bion 1962: 36)

Holding everything, unconditional acceptance of all that flies her way: in psychoanalytic and in everyday imagery, this is a mother's task. And the father? He is nowhere to be seen. Not now the conquering hero, more the shrivelled worm. The Kleinian mother may be a martyr, but at least she has guts.

'Do you share your upset with your husband?' I ask. 'No, what for? He says not to think about it, it won't change things. Anyway, he gets upset himself and he can't stand that.' So she protects him by her silence: if he cannot do anything about their suffering, it is better not to speak about it at all. Also, if he gets upset he goes into a rage, so it is better if she shoulders the whole thing herself.

THE NURTURING MAN

Perhaps it is not surprising that there have been some theoretical developments in psychoanalysis aimed at constructing alternative images of the father as someone who might be more than a prohibitive force, yet be a force of some kind. One major input comes from the feminist psychoanalyst Julia Kristeva, whose work 'embodies' both the male principles of Lacan and the female perspectives of Klein. Taking up the Kleinian assumption that the mother incorporates all the phallic elements of the father, making them her own, Kristeva argues that, while the pre-Oedipal mother is certainly phallic in the sense of being the focus of all the infant's desire, there is something outside her from the start, something towards which the mother can look, preventing her from falling into total absorption in, and identification with, her child. For Kristeva, this 'something' is termed the 'father of individual prehistory', or the 'archaic inscription of the father'.

The father of individual prehistory is presented by Kristeva as a pre-Oedipal entity, operating in the context of the mother – specifically as an object towards which the mother can look, turning her desire away from the infant, and so creating a space into which that infant can grow. Kristeva writes that,

> The loving mother, different from the caring and clinging mother, is someone who has an object of desire; beyond that, she has an Other with relation to whom the child will serve as a go-between... Without the maternal 'diversion' towards a Third Party, the bodily exchange is abjection or devouring.
>
> (Kristeva 1983: 251)

In Lacanian thought, the mother is always partly structured by the law of the father, as an entity both in, and at the boundaries of, the Symbolic. But here, Kristeva is working with an idea of the mother as *subject* in a different sense – as having something which is her own (a desire for another) that offers her a space which is also her own (she is not defined solely in terms of her mothering function or, as Kleinians imply, as already encompassing the father), and that also makes it possible for the infant to resist being submerged in her closeness and immediacy. In relation to the father, Kristeva opposes the Lacanian implication of a fixed symbolic order defined by the phallus and by the paternal 'non' (fatherhood as a prohibiting function). Instead, she argues for the importance of a more heterogeneous experience of the father – both in the Imaginary and in the Symbolic, something that creates a supportive space and that also makes symbolic regulation and expression possible. Here, for example, is her argument concerning the way the use of symbols promotes the 'triumph over sadness' necessary for recovery from depression. What makes this possible, she writes, is the ability of the individual to identify with something other than the lost object – a traditionally Oedipal scenario. However, this outside figure or 'Third Party' is enabling rather than prohibitive, preventing the subject from being engulfed by the lost object. As such, the third party is the 'imaginary father' who functions in exactly this way – creating a space for the infant's subjectivity – in earliest development. Nevertheless, writes Kristeva:

it is imperative that this father in individual prehistory be capable of playing his part as oedipal father in symbolic Law, for it is on the basis of that harmonious blending of the two facets of father-hood that the abstract and arbitrary signs of communication may be fortunate enough to be tied to the affective meaning of pre-historical identifications, and the dead language of the poten-tially depressive person can arrive at a live meaning in the bond with others.

(Kristeva 1987: 23–4)

As Elizabeth Grosz (1992) points out, this is an image of the imaginary father as embodying love – contributing to the ambiva-lence with which many feminists regard Kristeva, as it seems to suggest that the father is superior to the mother in this respect, and more generally that subjectivity can only be secured with the assistance of a patriarchal structure protecting the child against maternal engulfment. However, Kristeva's approach here can equally be seen as a plea for a reinstatement of a different notion of fathering from that defined solely by domination – and she specifically notes that it is only in the combination of the imaginary father with the Oedipal one, that symbolic activity can become truly alive.

For Jessica Benjamin, writing within a different psychoanalytic tradition from that espoused by Kristeva, the urgency of construc-ting a new rendering of the father is equally great. Opposing the theoretical emphasis on gender dimorphism, she argues that chil-dren construct much more complex relationships and internal worlds than is often recognised, in particular through processes of identification and identificatory love with parents of both sexes. Where Benjamin's emphasis differs from that of classical psycho-analysis is in her portrayal of the possibility of a pre- or non-Oedipal identificatory love for the father which is nurturing and productive, and which makes it possible for object-love to occur without (in the case of the boy) necessitating repudiation of the mother and her associated femininity.

Identificatory love has been, wrongly I think, assimilated to the boy's negative Oedipus complex, conflating the boy's homoerotic wish to be loved by father as like him with the heteroerotic wish to be to father as the mother is. Actually, these are pretty much obverse relationships to father. The negative Oedipus, I suggest, represents a movement *from* identification *to* object love, paralleling the positive Oedipal movement from identification to object love of the opposite sex. However, in the negative Oedipal case the boy renounces identification with father not because of the ineluctable dictates of gender, but because of parental impediments in the way of the identificatory paternal bond.

(Benjamin 1995: 113)

The capacity to love and to form identifications with the opposite sex can be built up on the basis of a heterogeneous pattern of identifications which include loving ones with a father who offers something positive. The father therefore represents not just a space towards which the mother turns, as in Kristeva's gloss, and certainly not just an Oedipal prohibition. What Benjamin seems to be suggesting is that the active presence of a loving father, unafraid of the threat of the young child – perhaps particularly the boy – is what will give that child the capacity to surmount loss and become integrated in relationships with others. On the other hand, this loving relationship can be blocked by the actions of the father – by 'impediments' caused by repudiation of the intense identificatory bond. Countering this, identifications can and should be 'over-inclusive' in a radical sense: that they take in everything available.

[To] the degree that the characteristics of the other have been lovingly incorporated through identification in the over-inclusive phase, loss can be ameliorated and the sequelae of the Oedipal phase can be informed more by other-love than by repudiation/idealisation.

(Benjamin 1995: 114)

It is not that the father must offer to the child exactly what is offered by the mother; rather, he should not be afraid to offer what he can.

Sam's father has stayed at home with Sam since his mother died, not sending the boy to school. 'I want to be everything to him now,' he says, 'but people tell me he will cope with the separation; they say I should send him to school.' I think, I wish nobody had to go to school. Perhaps people's criticism of Sam's father reflects their discomfort with – and their envy of – his decision not to act in accordance with what Sam might 'cope' with, but with what he and Sam want.

PATERNAL IDENTITY

The question arises from all this theorising: What resonance might it have for men? It is perhaps no accident that the two major psychoanalytic theorists of an enlarged notion of fathering quoted above are both women. They are clearer about what is needed, can see the gaps in girls' and boys' experiences created by the presence and the conceptualisation of a purely negative, constraining father. This does not mean that no work is going on amongst men (see, for example, Samuels 1994), but whereas Kristeva and Benjamin carve out a clear arena for debate from within a firm critique of psychoanalytic theory, men are struggling with their – our – ambivalence.

If there is a crisis in masculinity at the present time, it presumably resides somewhere in the relation between the collapse of traditional men's work, the growth of a technological culture which cannot be 'passed on' in any recognisable way between the generations, the rise of feminist consciousness amongst women, and the disconnections introduced into the modes of rationality with which masculinity has been identified, at least in the west (see, for example, Seidler 1994; Segal 1990; Frosh 1994). It also, as Christopher Lasch pointed out some time ago and as the Frankfurt School theorists realised even before that (Lasch, 1979; Marcuse, 1955), has to do with a crisis of authority that places men in a strained, even impossible, position with regard to received ideas on fathering. The term used by Marcuse was the 'administered society': whereas personal modes of authority, located symbolically in the father, were once the channel for communication and incorporation of values and inhibitions, under the conditions of modernity these are replaced by bureaucratised and anonymous modes, to which the father is as much the uncomprehending subject as is his child. The father then acts in the spirit of authority, but what he communicates is primarily his impotence. With very few exceptions, and those are media-supported fantasies, no-one can embody authority; there is no longer an Oedipal father available to any of us, for as we approach him, or try to become him, we find that he is being worked by some unseen hands.

Nowadays, in the context of what has come to be called post-modernist culture, there is even more confusion around – and not just amongst theorists and cultural critics. Whereas the father might once have acted as if he was representative of, and spokesman for, social values and the power of an inherited system, it is now harder to know which if any of the many available alternative heritages to select as the one to which oneself and one's children should belong. Or rather, turning this formulation on its head, the multiplicity of transient, superficial and incomprehensible micro-narratives of experience, which each of us sees displayed before us, is more likely to lead to the narcissism of unfocused marginality than to anything resembling belongingness. Under these conditions, paternity ceases to operate as a psychological process of transmitting culture to the next generation: all that any person can pass on to anyone else is confusion.

Where the crisis of masculinity intersects with the crisis of fathering, then, is in the difficulty men have in positioning ourselves within any meaningful set of discourses. Not only is it hard to become the nurturing pre-Oedipal father, created *de novo* from the absence of any received model of such fathering, but it is even difficult to sustain any sense of being a prohibitive father, enforcing social values. What is the result of this? Confusion, inconsistency, obsessionality and narcissistic rage. One response is to worry about it, another to aggressively attack the fantasised source of the destruction of inner identity – the mother and the feminine 'other'.

Most psychoanalytic theorists of the contemporary crisis of masculinity have focused on the way masculine identity is forged as a negative, as a movement away from something intimate and known – the relationship with the (admittedly idealised) mother – towards something more abstract, much less available and knowable: the father whose voice is heard, but who is, emotionally and therefore concretely, much less present in the boy's life. As a consequence, masculine identity is a search rather than a foundation, defined largely in terms of what it is not – it is not what the mother represents; it is anything but her. Here are some comments on this, from a man and two women.

> Belonging is a male problem in our existing system of man and woman, 'masculinity' and 'femininity'; it is the obsession of my identity as a man, getting things straight, knowing where I am and what I have and where she is and what she hasn't.
>
> (Heath 1987: 16)

> The man's anal game comes down to this: how to stop the other from existing, how to remove all trace of her desire, how to kill her in fantasy.
>
> (Olivier 1980: 64)

The vulnerability of masculinity that is forged in the crucible of femininity, the 'great task' of separation that is so seldom completed, lays the groundwork for the later objectification of women. The mother stands as the prototype of the undifferentiated object. She serves men as their other, their counterpart, the side of themselves they repress.

(Benjamin 1988: 77)

The aggression attributed to men in this material is palpable, an aggression presumably serving the function of defending men against the feeling that they (we) have no substance. Faced with a dissolving gender identity, men often retreat into *more* fantasy masculinity, anywhere that will take us away from the world of the mother, the world of dependence, intimacy and boundary loss. One consequence of this retreat can be an attempt to drum up a mythical past in which men had something to pass on to one another (Bly 1990); another could be abusiveness, direct translation of aggression into physical and sexual violence, towards women or – finally back to the subject – towards children (Jukes 1993; Frosh 1994).

The irony is a strong one here: psychoanalysis suggests that children need not just a prohibitive Oedipal father, but a nurturing pre-Oedipal one, able to offer a loving space to the mother (object relations and Kristevan theory) and a direct source of gratification to the child (Benjamin). Psychoanalysis also suggests that masculine gender identity is built largely on the repudiation of precisely those characteristics which might make this loving fathering possible: the boy child is thought to turn away from the mother and from all she represents (dependence, intimacy, bodily absorption) in order to carve out a separate existence in the shadow of the absent father. Too much closeness to the maternal leads to dissolution of masculine identity; moreover, the more fragile the sources of this identity – for instance, because of social conditions militating against secure identity formation – the more vivid and vicious this repudiation can become. Hence the specific complexity of the ambivalence surrounding fathering: to father a child requires something other than the traditional boundary-setting and prohibitive stance, as no authority is vested in the father to sustain that stance; but to reach out in a loving way requires a shift of masculine consciousness, involving not just some more gentleness but a whole gamut of alterations in relations of dependency, intimacy, vulnerability and trust. On the whole, the more fragile masculinity becomes, the more desperately men cling to its vestiges, doing the opposite of what fathering requires.

There is a rather pessimistic outlook from this point. As the conditions spawned by late modernity produce lives lived in fragments, it is less likely than ever that boys will experience the kinds of secure, stable and intimate relationships that might allow them sufficient stability of selfhood to be able to reach out to others, rather than flee from – or attack – them. Yet children will continue to make demands for precisely this reaching-out, for parenting which will hold them together in the face of fragmenting tendencies which (whether or not they also come from within, as psychoanalysis postulates) certainly come from without. If Kleinians are right in conceptualising the parenting task along maternal lines as a holding, containing and feeding-back enterprise tolerant of all the excesses of the child's impulses; and if the post-Kleinians mentioned in this chapter are correct in adding to this a paternal function which is primarily libidinal and loving rather than prohibitive and disconnecting, then fathers are faced with the same kind of impossible task that mothers have always had to face. But in facing that task they do not start from the same point. Expecting to be looked after but fearful of dependency, men who become fathers must struggle with the gap between their own fathers' emotional absence and their own needy response. As their children make increasingly urgent demands, so these men often find themselves – ourselves, of course – fluctuating wildly between caricatures of the prohibitive patriarch (do as I say) and the overinvolved mother. What is hardest of all to do is to find a way of meeting the child's actual demand for presence, calm, and thoughtful love.

Is there an 'optimism of the will' to be rescued from this pessimism of the intellect? As with all gross oversimplifications, there are many instances of resistive practice to be found in everyday life that contradict the assertions here: Men who are present for their children, who do offer a loving space, who are not terrified of renouncing something which might once have been called 'masculinity', and who are not too afraid of being inconsistent at different times and in differing places. What makes these resistive practices possible is the fact that experience is not seamless, that everyone's 'take' on parenting is different. Some men have had fathers who were present for them; others have partners who offer them a security they can pass on; many have had mothers whom they admire and whose love they replicate with their own children. These features of experience, gendered and cross-gendered, can be internalised, identified with, owned and repeated with those men's own children. Many men pity themselves but some pity their children more, and are shocked by the terrors in the world into offering the kind of protective space which children might need. Some men even feel good about themselves in a relatively non-narcissistic way, and make their children feel good too. Most do not, it is probably true; but some do, some do.

> 'I'm thinking of sending him to his father,' Elizabeth said. 'He needs something from him even if he can't give it.' 'But I don't want to go,' said the boy. 'He hits me even more than you do. Anyway, it's funny when you're angry; it's not funny at all with him.'

Certainty is almost always destructive; ambivalence has many positive attributes. For fathers, the conundrum around closeness versus distance, intimacy versus independence, can only be resolved through the apocryphal third term, the synthesis itself. What is this synthesis? As a father, I do not know.

REFERENCES

Benjamin, J. (1988) *The Bonds of Love*, London: Virago, 1990.
Benjamin, J. (1995) 'Sameness and Difference: Toward an "Over-inclusive" Theory of Gender Development', in A. Elliott and S. Frosh (eds) *Psychoanalysis in Contexts*, London: Routledge.
Bion, W. (1962) *Learning from Experience*, London: Maresfield.
Bly, R. (1990) *Iron John*, Brisbane: Element.
Freud, S. (1939) 'Moses and Monotheism', in S. Freud, *The Origins of Religion*, Harmondsworth: Penguin, 1985.
Frosh, S. (1987) *The Politics of Psychoanalysis*, London: Macmillan.
Frosh, S. (1994) *Sexual Difference: Masculinity and Psychoanalysis*, London: Routledge.
Grosz, E. (1992) 'Kristeva, Julia', in E. Wright (ed.) *Feminism and Psychoanalysis: A Critical Dictionary*, Oxford: Blackwell.
Grunberger, B. (1989) *New Essays on Narcissism*, London: Free Association Books.
Heath, S. (1987) 'Male Feminism', in A. Jardine and P. Smith (eds) *Men in Feminism*, London: Methuen.
Hinshelwood, R. (1989) *A Dictionary of Kleinian Thought*, London: Free Association Books.

Jukes, A. (1993) *Why Men Hate Women*, London: Free Association Books.
Kristeva, J. (1983) 'Freud and Love', in T. Moi (ed.) *The Kristeva Reader*, Oxford: Blackwell.
—— (1987) *Black Sun*, New York: Columbia University Press, 1989.
Lacan, J. (1955/1956) *The Seminars of Jacques Lacan, Book 2*, Cambridge: Cambridge University Press.
Lasch, C. (1979) *The Culture of Narcissism*, London: Abacus.
Marcuse, H. (1955) *Eros and Civilisation*, Boston: Beacon Press, 1966.
Olivier, C. (1980) *Jocasta's Children*, London: Routledge, 1989.
Samuels, A. (1994) *The Political Psyche*, London: Routledge.
Segal, H. (1973) *Introduction to the Work of Melanie Klein*, London: Hogarth Press.
Segal, L. (1990) *Slow Motion: Changing Masculinities, Changing Men*, London: Virago.
Seidler, V. (1994) *Unreasonable Men*, London: Routledge.

Chapter 4

The maternal bed

Wendy Hollway

THE PARENTAL BED

Until my daughter was 7 years old, her father and I slept together in a capacious and comfortable bed, which was a significant part of her world from when she was newborn. In the night, she was fed there and, if she couldn't settle, stayed and slept there. She had her morning feed there, while we drank tea in bed and started the day, the three of us, a small family.[1] Later, when she was old enough to have a single bed and big enough for our bed to feel cramped with three in it, there were occasions when she would come in with one of us while the other one slept in her bed for the rest of the night. That was part of shared child care. It was flexible and for the most part unproblematic. It reflected the central position she had in our triangular relationship, the only and much-treasured child. The clear assumption, however, was that it was the parental bed; that is, that big bed symbolised the impossibility of her turning into reality the phantasy of displacing either of us from our privileged relationship with each other. Having said that, her place when she was there was usually between us.

I am starting here because I want to emphasise the inevitable significations of the parental bed as they develop from earliest infancy and become reworked later, through cultural knowledge about sex and gender, mediated by phantasies. In contemporary British culture, probably across the classes, the double bed is a standard and taken-for-granted symbol of the privileges accruing to the adult couple: privileges of sex, intimacy, closeness, comfort, attention and, in an important sense, being put first; that is, before the children. More precisely, though, the double bed will function as a marker through which the special (sexual) significance of the adult couple is learned: sexual intercourse is understood, sooner or later, as the act that happens between the parents when the child is not there, and to that extent it must signify as an exclusion based on generational difference:

> What the child has to accept is not primarily the prohibition of his incestuous wishes, but the reality of his position in relation to his parent's sexual relationship.
>
> (Temperley 1993: 271)

The profound emotional significance of the privileges associated with the parental bed was expressed in Freud's concept of the 'primal scene', his way of referring to the knowledge of the parents' sexual intercourse, a mixture of phantasy and reality. In his theorisation of Oedipal dynamics, the insight was extended to the proposition that the father – the third term – is necessary to come between the mother and child. However, his understanding of these issues was forged through personal and clinical experience of a middle-class, middle-European, nineteenth-century culture in which the parental bed was a hallowed place where the patriarch had exclusive rights over his wife (rights which were not symmetrical). If the nanny could not cater for the children's requirements, mother went to the nursery to tend them there.[2] Meanwhile, across Europe and beyond, labouring families were crammed together in the only bedroom, and maybe the only bed, in the house. Similarly, cultures where women and children are separately accommodated, where men visit their wives, will have generated different meanings. Children's knowledge of sex between the parents is bound to differ, but in every case, according to psychoanalysis, phantasies will powerfully mediate the reality to influence a girl's or boy's developing subjectivity. The incest taboo is, by all accounts, universal, and that anthropological fact will profoundly influence all cultures and all sexual practices (Lévi-Strauss 1969; Mitchell 1974).

Psychoanalysis has frequently been accused of universalism, particularly in relation to the Oedipus complex and the related ideas of penis envy and castration. If there now exist parent–child dynamics which do not so readily mirror the patriarchal relations recognised in Freud's theorising of the Oedipus complex, will this have significant effects? Psychoanalysis has been quite elusive on the issue of how changing external realities, both historical and cultural, affect the entry of children into gendered subjectivity. The common criticism that Freud's scenario was treated as universal but was in fact culturally and historically specific[3] has been dealt with by psycho-analysis insisting that children's understandings are not simple reflections of external reality but complexly mediated by phantasies which, in their turn, are archaic reflections of the dominant culture. Benjamin, for example, clarifies:

> I think that differences in psychic development that result from specific social arrangements of personal life have to be under-stood against the background of the dominant culture and its gender structure, as represented by an abstract model of personal and sexual life. The figures of mother and father are cultural ideals, but they need not be played by 'biological' mothers and fathers, or even women and men.
>
> (Benjamin 1990a: 105 fn)

Given these 'abstract models' which exist in the psyche but are related to the dominant culture, what differences will it make if women bring up children on their own, or in lesbian relationships, or with a long-term surrogate parent, or in a succession of sexual relationships, or where the father's physical presence has become equally associated with the meeting of a child's needs for care and attention or where both parents (or partners) appear to privilege and respect each other equally?

In this chapter, I show how the emphasis on object relations, which prefigure Oedipal relations and are implicated within them, gives a richer understanding of the tasks facing children and par-ents. I try to show that the classical psychoanalytic view of the achievement of gendered subjectivity derives from an illegitimate overvaluation of the effects of Oedipal dynamics and a consequent emphasis on difference, in contrast to pre-Oedipal dynamics (or early Oedipal dynamics, according to Klein), particularly in con-nection with parental nurturing and authority.

I start by trying to convey, in psychodynamic language and using my own experience as a parent, the significance to the child of its parents breaking up and, more importantly, of what happens then. I then consider the congruence between Oedipal theory and 'families need fathers' discourse. If there are now theoretically viable cri-tiques of, and alternatives to, classical Oedipal theory, then it is important to explore what their implications are for the belief – deeply embedded within western cultures – that families need fathers. I therefore present a short critical account of Oedipal theory, drawing on the following feminist critiques: the failure to account for girls' moral development; the uncritical valorisation of paternal authority as a force for (masculine) moral development; the lack of an independent maternal subjectivity or an infantile capacity to pursue differentiation from the mother; the overdrawn assumption that Oedipal dynamics cancel out pre-Oedipal developments; the commitment to difference as exclusive of similarity; the conflation of the acquisition of gender identity with sexual object choice.

In different ways, Jessica Benjamin's work and that of Melanie Klein and subsequent Kleinians provide alternative accounts, without ignoring the importance of Oedipal conflicts for the child's development. I briefly outline the different emphases of a Kleinian account which stresses the inseparability of Oedipal dynamics from the achievement of an integrated self in the depressive position. I then use Benjamin, who theorises the continuing importance of an autonomous mother, capable of recognition, in the child's capacity to differentiate; the child itself becomes capable of recognition and therefore capable of retaining good maternal identifications, whatever its sex. I then introduce the Kleinian emphasis on the importance of the parental relationship in the infant's mind, and the use of the parental relationship in the baby's coming to terms with reality and forging its subjectivity, through experiences of existing within triangular space. While I believe that Oedipal dynamics are, in some sense, universal, I try to show that there are practical implications for the parenting which takes place in different family constellations, including the ever-more common triangle of mother–child–mother's lover.

THE MATERNAL BED

Let me return to my story. When my daughter was 7, the commonplace thing happened. Her father left. She stayed mostly with me for quite a while. We were all devastated. Probably most parents in such situations try to explain to our children that he (she) has left, not because he doesn't love them any more, but because he doesn't love Mum (Dad) any more. Probably this makes little impact on their fears. After all, Dad (Mum) *did* leave them too. How do they know that the other one will not similarly desert them? These fears are made worse when new sexual partners are on the scene, as they often are. People typically leave relationships, not only when they are dissatisfied, but when they find someone else to 'fall in love with'. This gives them the courage to leave and meets their dependency needs. Trust in adults' love has already taken a battering and then the child is presented with a new twist: Dad (Mum) has chosen this stranger over the other parent. For the child who loves both its parents, it must be difficult to grasp that adults can love a stranger more. If a child identifies with the deserted parent, her/his experience is of losing a parent to a stranger (or relative stranger) whom the parent loves more than he/she loves the child. When visits and access are arranged, typically the parent's new partner is there, maybe anxious quickly to become accepted as a surrogate parent, maybe jealous. The effect is not only to deny the importance of trust and familiarity built up over a lifetime, but also to expect the child to relate to a new unit (in which the parent now is), rather than to a familiar parent (which he/she would be without the new partner). Often, if it is the father who has gone, family, friends and officials encourage this settling down with a new partner, guided by an assumption that a man on his own is incapable of providing a home for his child/children.

All this makes the behaviour of the remaining parent of enormous importance to the child's ability to feel secure: Can that parent be trusted to remain the same; not to be transformed by this mysterious process of 'loving' which leads to desertion? At this time, however, the parent who is left behind is probably feeling – as I was – rejected, vulnerable, lonely and vindictive. Given the way that intimacy is usually only expected and sought in a sexual relationship, it is common that the deserted parent quickly finds solace in a new sexual relationship. This might last a night or a lifetime, but will likely be witnessed very soon by the child(ren).

I did not remain unattached for long. When my new lover was still almost a stranger to my daughter, she had to come to terms with the experience of him in my bed; that same bed that had been the family bed; that same bed to which, on many a night when she woke feeling fearful or lonely, she would come to get comfort from my peaceful, sleeping presence[4] and where she could wake with me in the morning. I never discouraged this, but now there were times when the presence of this imposter must have seemed to prohibit it. She was torn between the desire for my comforting presence in the maternal bed and the discomfort of a resented, unfamiliar intruder. I think that she lived in dread of him moving in, and her resistance settled into familiar forms, while I patiently hoped, as he did, that she would 'accept' him eventually.

Such common occurrences raise questions which bear upon the debate concerning the damage done to children following the break-up of their parents' relationship. The panic about lone mothers rarely pauses long enough to think about whether a woman is really on her own with the children, or with a succession of boyfriends (or women sexual partners).[5] Those articulating a 'families need fathers' discourse rarely reflect on what kind of father, or surrogate father, is better than no father at all.[6] In a political climate characterised by a panic about the connections between lone mothering and children's (especially boys') moral decline, it is important that feminists take seriously the parental conditions for bringing up children who have the capacity to love and respect others. While material conditions are undoubtedly influential in child rearing – especially of course, the provision of good child-care facilities for single, and other, mothers who, from choice or necessity, go out to work – I am convinced they are not determining.

While the recent political and popular rhetoric of 'families need fathers' has lacked an articulated intellectual underpinning, in 1977 Christopher Lasch's *Haven in a Heartless World* spoke to a similar crisis in the United States, where it was influential in articulating the belief that the loss of the traditional (nuclear) family undermined children's healthy psychological development (see Sayers 1995). Importantly for this analysis, Lasch based his arguments on Freud's account of the necessity of Oedipal conflict in children's development – a conflict which depended on a father who exercised traditional paternal authority: 'Lasch's romantic view of the psychological strengths derived from the Oedipal conflict underlies his general support for authoritarian styles of socialisation' (Barrett and McIntosh 1982: 119).[7]

Freud's account of the passage of the child through Oedipal conflict is, as Lasch demonstrates, powerfully supportive of a 'families need fathers' position. It is also the cornerstone of orthodox Freudian psychoanalysis as well as of Lacanian and some feminist developments. For these reasons, it is important to consider alternative readings and meanings of Oedipal theory, bearing in mind that none is definitive and all are part of a struggle to influence common sense.

OEDIPAL CONFLICTS

A newborn infant is totally dependent and usually its first, most intense and most sustained relationship is with its natural mother:

from womb, to breast and beyond – towards the necessity of a subjectivity differentiated from hers, and desires that are not still hooked into her as their object. This is where Oedipus starts, in the anxious attempt to cope with the necessity of separation. While there could be many strands in a resolution of this developmental challenge, the conventional Oedipal story has it that the father is necessary for this separation to be accomplished, to come between mother and child. Underlying Freud's account is the assumption that mothers and children between them cannot enable the kind of separation which is necessary for subsequent adult development.[8] Mothers in this formulation are as narcissistically attached to children as children would be to mothers if the father did not intervene (see Benjamin 1994). By this account there is nothing else sufficient in the lives of women who are mothers, no other 'third term', to produce their independence from their children. By this account also, single mothers would produce children who were incapable of growing up to be autonomous, bereft of moral responsibility. This fear – often for fatherless boys – is reflected in the contemporary 'families need fathers' discourse.

In the process of extricating itself from dependence (a psychic dependence in which the experiences of the infant, its mental objects and thus its fledgling subjectivity are at the mercy of a maternal figure, powerful both in phantasy and reality), the infant phantasises that it is omnipotent; that it can exercise whatever control it wishes over the maternal object in order to satisfy its desires. Such phantasies will continuously be subjected to reality tests in relation to the real mother: tests whose outcome can be influenced by the child in its struggle to control its mother's desires. There are two kinds of rival for the mother: her activities and – a threat of a different order – her other relationships. I have experienced powerful resistance from my daughter across both of these fronts, with issues of control and autonomy being worked out in the process. Of the mother's other relationships, the sexual partner, if there is one, is the most significant.[9] It is in the sense of the child facing life beyond dyadic dependence – facing it in its most rivalrous form – that I consider the concept of Oedipus to be of central importance to the development of subjectivity.

The principle which seems to survive all critiques of the Oedipal model is that the three-person or triangular relationship of child–mother–father is characterised by competition (for the mother), jealousy (especially the child's) and superior power (of the parents, but particularly of the father). An indispensable criterion for the utility of such a theory is that it must be capable of illuminating the development of gender differences and of the object of desire and its sexualisation.

Since the father and mother signify differently to girl and boy children because of gender difference, the processes whereby this separation is accomplished (and their effects) will be different for sons and daughters. Oedipal conflicts are happening at a relatively late stage (the fourth year, in Freudian theory), when boys and girls are having to come to terms with genital difference and more importantly with genital difference as a marker for gender difference.[10] It is impossible for the child to triumph in this rivalry over the father, except in phantasy. The sexual partner is privileged in numerous ways: if it is a man, he has a unique position in the family structure, a gendered and generational one. Moreover, he is meant, in this structure, to have exclusive claim on the mother's sexuality, and certainly sex is meant to be proscribed across generations (the incest taboo). It is within such meaning structures, based on generational and gender power difference, that sexual desire comes to signify for the developing child and to affect its developing (gendered) subjectivity: 'reality lies in the differences of sex and generation' (Chasseguet-Smirgel, quoted in Bassin, Honey and Mahrer Kaplan 1994: 115).

The impossibility of triumphing over the father provides the push towards identification with him: by putting itself in the father's place, the child can imagine itself as object of its mother's desire.[11] This identification supposedly provides an escape from maternal dependence and establishes the boy's own super-ego. However, as is evident here, the story only really works for the boy: because of gender difference, the girl experiences obstacles to her identification with the father and has to forge a different route. One argument in this chapter is that these obstacles need not be there, if identifications with both parents (for girls and boys) have not been given up on account of Oedipal dynamics. (See also Benjamin 1995a.)

In consequence of the way the Oedipal account is gendered, features of adult autonomy, moral responsibility and independence end up as a product of the father's intervention into the narcissistic mother–son dyad. This is why the classical Oedipal account supports a 'families need fathers' discourse (in which, as in Oedipal theory, girls' development is elided with boys'). As Stephanie Engel argues in her critique of Lasch:

That women must choose to love an individual of the opposite sex when their primary love relationship would prepare them only for narcissistic object relations was a problem Freud never resolved... traits such as dependence, immaturity, rigidity and masochism have been conflated under the analytic umbrella of 'narcissism', the psychological trademark of femininity.

(Engel quoted in Barrett and McIntosh 1982: 124)

Does the Oedipal triangle privilege boys' acquisition of an autonomous subjectivity which sets the standard for moral responsibility and family leadership? With what gains and losses of potential and autonomy do girls achieve a gendered subjectivity (by this I mean more than acquiring 'femininity')? The girl is expected to achieve a love of difference despite her original love-object being the same sex as she is. Moreover, she is expected to achieve this love of difference based on experience of a paternal object who may be physically or emotionally absent and poor at providing recognition for a daughter. His own masculinity, his difference from her, may be 'forged as a negative' (see Frosh, Chapter 3). If she does turn to her father, and if later she reproduces similar dynamics with a male sexual partner, her tendency to idealise this object makes sense in terms of how little reality testing she has probably been able to do in her relationship to a real father. Phantasies of the other – of split-off, unacceptable parts of herself – will fill the reality void. In this account, the real father (who may be the original father, the mother's sexual partner, or both, see note 16) makes a difference.

The orthodox Oedipal account is motivated by a commitment to the desirability of gender *difference* – it would seem at whatever psychic cost. This difference is seen as mutually exclusive characteristics derived from either the father or the mother, with the others given up during the Oedipal phase (see Benjamin 1995a). Conventional Oedipal accounts also presume that the developments that precede this stage (pre-Oedipal dynamics which are centred on infant and mother) are cancelled out by the trauma of Oedipal conflict. Klein disagreed with this assumption: 'There is no doubt in my mind as to the far-reaching and lasting influence of every facet of the relation to the mother upon the relation to the father' (Klein 1945: 418).

Klein also disagreed that the development of conscience or morality depended on the establishment of a strong super-ego. On the contrary, through her clinical work she found that the early super-ego was usually savage, much harsher than the standards exacted by real parental figures and that this led to such high anxiety that its consequences were inconsistent with the development of conscience: 'anxiety will serve to increase [the child's] own sadistic impulses' (Klein 1933: 251), which in turn increase anxiety. Klein's conclusion has radical implications for child rearing, as it has for the Freudian underpinning of Lasch's argument: 'we must assume that it is the excessive severity and overpowering cruelty of the super-ego, not the weakness or want of it, as is usually supposed, which is responsible for the behaviour of asocial and criminal persons' (ibid.).

KLEIN'S OEDIPUS

Although Klein is often regarded as having theorised pre-Oedipal relations at the expense of Oedipal ones, subsequent writers in a Kleinian tradition (for example, Temperley 1993; Britton 1992, 1993) have shown this to be far from the case. For Klein, Oedipal dynamics start much earlier than for Freud, in the second half of the first year of life. They develop contemporaneously with the early working through of the depressive position[12] and only culminate with the 'classical' Oedipus in the fourth year. According to Britton:

> The Oedipus situation dawns with the child's recognition of the parents' relationship in whatever primitive or partial form. It is continued by the child's rivalry with one parent for the other, and it is resolved by the child relinquishing his sexual claim on his parents by his acceptance of the reality of their sexual relationship.
>
> (Britton 1993: 83)

I shall be arguing that, depending on how this relinquishing is accomplished, the classical resolution of Oedipal conflicts can be understood as a failure to work through the depressive position (in the crucial arena of parental relationships), rather than the achievement of a mature step into differentiation and individuation. In contrast, in Kleinian theory 'the Oedipus complex is not bad news for women but the possibility both of autonomy and of a sexual relationship to men which respects and avails itself creatively of difference' (Temperley 1993: 273).

Britton (1992, 1993), following Klein, stresses that Oedipal dynamics and those associated with the working through of the depressive position occur at the same time in infant development.

This working through[13] means the achievement of the capacity to recognise conflicting feelings (love and hate) and objects (good and bad) as belonging to the same, integrated person. It centrally involves the acknowledgement of ambivalence (see Parker, Chapter 2). Britton makes the point that acknowledging the existence of an integrated mother also requires that 'the mother perceived as a feeding and loving mother has to be perceived as the same person as the sexual mother' (1992: 39). If so, we are talking about the incipient triangular relationship, involving the mother, as well as the father, being perceived as sexual, if not in reality, then in the child's phantasy. Loss is entailed by the acknowledgement of reality; an acknowledgement which characterises moves from the paranoid-schizoid position to the depressive position: loss of the experience of 'timeless bliss' characteristic of the early infantile state of satisfaction when it is still split from frustration; loss of the phantasy of omnipotence, of control of the good object. However, when the sexual mother is recognised as being one and the same as the feeding, loving mother, not only loss but envy is involved: the envy of the sexual relationship that the child cannot hope to rival, except in the future. Here, the primary dynamic is not a gendered, but a generational one.

THE AUTONOMOUS MOTHER

Feminism's recent contribution to the mothering debate is marked by constructing an autonomous subjectivity for mothers. It insists on seeing them as more than mothers as well as more than the images of mothers – whether idealising or denigrating – which characterise past and contemporary cultures (Thurer 1994; Kaplan 1992; Dally 1982). To help understand the motivational construction of this autonomous mother, Jessica Benjamin uses a feminist psychoanalytic tradition (notably Chodorow) which emphasises connectedness and differentiation, particularly stressing these processes within the mother–child dyad. She develops feminist object relations theory in two directions which are relevant here. Firstly, she talks not only about the mother's need to be a subject, but the child's need for the mother's independent subjectivity. This is based on a model of intersubjectivity (Benjamin 1990b) stressing the capacity for mutual recognition between child and mother. Secondly, she addresses the 'fatherless society' critics (Benjamin 1978, 1981), and engages in a critique of Oedipal theory (Benjamin 1990a, 1995a). I shall first outline the way that these arguments offer an alternative to the internalisation of paternal authority as the route to autonomous subjectivity and then, in the following section, I shall supplement the feminist object relations focus on dyadic relationships with the Kleinian emphasis on the importance of Oedipal dynamics in producing a triangular space within which the infant will be situated.

Benjamin's argument for the necessity of a mother's independent subjectivity hinges on her linked notions of differentiation and recognition. Starting from the object relations premise that the infant is primarily object-seeking and only secondarily pleasure-seeking, Benjamin posits a conflict of differentiation, based on every infant's task of acquiring a self through differentiation from others, especially from the primary caretaker on whom she/he is dependent. The conflict is 'between the need to establish autonomous identity and the need to be recognised by the other' (Benjamin 1984: 293), a conflict which is, in my view, central to human motivation. The inherent tension between the need for differentiation and the need for recognition revolves around the paradox that 'the child's independent acts require a recognising audience and so reaffirm its dependency on others' (ibid.). In other words, in the act of differentiating, it is faced with its dependency on the other; need for the other's recognition.

This account has implications for how we understand the 'resolution' of Oedipal conflict, which revolves for boys around giving up the mother. An artificial resolution can be produced if the child imagines that it can be independent without recognising the other person as an equally autonomous agent; that is, without acknowledging that the other has independent desires and is not therefore under the child's omnipotent control. Boys will be particularly motivated to arrive at this 'false differentiation' because of the anxieties and threats of their Oedipal conflict. However, this solution is rendered unstable since the consequence of denying the other's independent subjectivity is that 'there is no-one to recognise us' (Benjamin 1984: 295; see also Hollway 1996). The dialectic of control consists in the dilemma that:

If I completely control the other, then the other ceases to exist, and if the other completely controls me, then I cease to exist. True differentiation means maintaining the essential tension of the contradictory impulses to assert the self and respect the other.
(Benjamin 1984: 295)

If the mother is denied as an autonomous agent (which is related to, but not determined by, the real mother) and therefore is experienced as incapable of recognising the child of either sex, who is left? In this perspective, the presence or absence of a father who is capable of love (see Frosh, Chapter 3) will be enormously important. The father may be incapable of love by being physically absent or emotionally absent, or he may be powerfully present with negative emotions, in which case the child is likely to deny his impact.[14] In any of these cases, he is incapable of affording recognition. The lack or loss of recognition from a mother will be particularly serious if there are no other close sources of recognition.

Benjamin's contribution resides primarily in her twin concepts of recognition and differentiation, especially in the mother's and child's developing capacities for these, interwoven and changing over time with the child's development. However, there is also an important space for the pre-Oedipal father in Benjamin's account. If, prior to the specific anxieties provoked by the Oedipal phase, the child of either sex has a relationship with the father based on recognition, then there is less pressure for a defensive resolution of Oedipal conflicts, a resolution marked by difference, idealisation and denigration – in other words, the perpetuation of unconscious phantasy. Rather, it is based on identificatory love in a real relationship, which is therefore generative as well as defensive (Benjamin, personal communication). The invocation of a pre-Oedipal father is to be found also in Kristeva's notion of the 'father of individual prehistory' (see Frosh, Chapter 3).[15] While not denying the importance of phantasy, I wish to argue that the relationship to a real father (as to a real mother)[16] makes an important difference to how girls and boys negotiate Oedipal conflicts, difficult though these may be.

According to a Freudian or Lacanian view, Oedipal conflicts erase pre-Oedipal dynamics in the child's developing psyche. Benjamin too recognises that Oedipal dynamics threaten the capacity of boys to preserve identifications with their mothers, and thus to preserve what will come to mean the 'feminine' parts of themselves. She suggests how 'the process of gender differentiation ... actually stalemates the potential recognition of subjectivity in the mother' (Benjamin 1994: 132). However, Oedipal dynamics are resolvable not only in defensive ways, but ways which draw on pre-Oedipal dynamics (in Kleinian terminology, depressive resolutions) as well as modifying them. Their outcome is affected by parental reality.

This emphasis is supported by recent clinical writings which, Breen suggests,

> stress the importance of the feminine component in men due to the early identification with the mother. This feminine identification is now understood as being not just a threat to masculinity but, more importantly, as potentially positive for intrapsychic development and interrelational balance
>
> (Breen 1993: 232)

Benjamin's critique lays bare the effects of an Oedipal theory which valorizes gender difference and defensive separation (1995a). She argues that, far from the boy's giving up the mother representing mature autonomous achievement of difference, it represents quite the opposite. This is because the mother is defensively 'repudiated' (through paternal power experienced as castration anxiety) rather than 'renounced' as part of the process of recognising the impossibility of taking the father's place and thus coming to terms with the reality of generational difference. The repudiation involves the psyche in projective processes – 'she *is* that thing I feel' – processes that 'intensify the fear of the other's omnipotence and the need to retaliate with assertion of one's own omnipotence' (Benjamin 1994: 133). In Kleinian terms, such processes would indicate a failure to reach or work through the depressive position; a regression to defences characteristic of the paranoid-schizoid position. Oedipal dynamics begin to sound more like a vicious defensive circle in which the child can remain incapable of achieving (or re-achieving) an undefensive differentiation. In Benjamin's view,

> the unaccepted mourning for that which one will never be – for instance the boy's inability to face the loss of not being the mother, to even acknowledge envy of the feminine – has particularly negative repercussions, more profound if less obvious than the classically recognised Oedipal frustration of not having mother.
>
> (Benjamin 1995a: 113)

Repudiation of the mother involves defensively rejecting recognition of the mother's power and independent subjectivity and also rejecting maternal identifications, because the dependency on the mother, and the desire for her, are too anxiety-provoking. This is the solution that Benjamin calls 'false differentiation', which is unstable because it is based on a defensive denial. In adults too: '[T]he insistence that the other be the heterosexual mirror image of the self, including intolerance of any other sexual elements, reflects a defence against envy, not an acceptance of difference' (Benjamin 1995a: 116). The implications of this argument are that rigid gender differentiation and homophobia and even 'normal masculinity' are unsuccessful attempts to come to terms with difference, as well as being disastrous in their acknowledgement of likeness. While what is referred to as 'Oedipus' may be a universal conflict, I see the resolution which produces defensive gender difference and rigid heterosexuality as an expression of the paranoid-schizoid position, a failure of integration, rather than a mature achievement of the autonomous ego.

In contrast, the dynamics that Benjamin is theorising permit another possible outcome of Oedipal conflicts:

> the wish to feel commonality and its concomitant, identificatory love, should alternate with recognising difference, and the concomitant object love. Identification could then be used to both ratify sameness and create commonality as a bridge across difference.
>
> (Benjamin 1995a: 115)

Here she is suggesting the possibility of identifications deriving from both parents which make up the character of children of either sex. Such outcomes contrast with the popular discourses which hark after a highly differentiated adult heterosexual couple, a couple which, as parents, produce a distant father who represents patriarchal authority and a merging mother who can provide no boundaries for her children (of either sex) because she is not sufficiently differentiated herself. However, the alternative as constructed by Benjamin, although stressing autonomous maternal subjectivity, does not mean that fathers are dispensable (I feel this is the unspoken fear mobilising the 'families need fathers' position). It does mean that the child's autonomous subjectivity, morality, capacity for relating, and relationship to their own sex and gender will be more affected by the quality of recognition provided by whatever adult carers provide continuous and reliable care. However, Benjamin's analysis stops at the two-person relationships that a child can have with parents and surrogate parents.[17] Kleinians add another dimension: triangular space, and by this means introduce maternal sexuality.

TRIANGULAR SPACE

The notion of triangular space provides a powerful way of conceptualising the shifts which an infant must make if it is to come to terms with reality beyond the mother. Initially the part-objects associated with the father are part of the baby's unconscious interpsychic communication with the mother (as in Klein's model of incorporation: see Frosh, Chapter 3). McDougall, for example, is convinced of 'the importance of the mother's unconscious projections upon the infant in the first year of life' (1993: 240). Within this unconscious dyad, 'of crucial importance is the place given to the baby's father in the mother's mind' (ibid.). Anna Freud likewise noted: 'I should add that part of the motivation to identify with the father stems from the mother's love and respect for the father. Identifications based on other grounds seem to be less reliable' (quoted in Greenson 1993: 263). This analysis renders all the more serious the widespread contempt, in Orbach's opinion, with which women regard their male partners (Orbach, Chapter 6). The place of the father (and/or other person in this position) in the mother's mind is one early step in what will later become the ability to recognise oneself in triangular relationships. Following this, relations with the mother and father (and/or whoever is there in a continuous relation with the infant) will begin to be separated from each other but experienced as two-person relationships; the child's with the mother and father, respectively. From here, the young child, beginning to confront Oedipal dynamics, will want to put itself between the parents. Only when the child accepts that the parents have a relationship independently of the child, which it does not control, can the triangle close. This is the meaning of castration for Temperley:

> For Kleinians, this transition involves the relinquishment of phantasies of omnipotent control of the object (through projective identification with it) and the acceptance of separateness ... It is the loss of this omnipotent control via projective identification which is the true 'realisation of castration'.
>
> (Temperley 1993: 273)

One of the most momentous consequences of the depressive position for the child is that it must come to terms not simply with the independent existence of its primary object, the mother, but the fact that the mother exists in relation to others as well as to the child. This is where Oedipal dynamics start, according to Kleinians. Whether these involve the actual mother or the actual father, the working through of the depressive position requires bringing these people together in the mind to create a 'triangular space': 'a space bounded by the three persons of the Oedipal situation and all their potential relationships' (Britton 1993: 84). This space includes awareness of the continuity of existence (others' as well as one's own) in time and space and expands the experience of reality for the child:

> the acknowledgement by the child of the parents' relationship with each other unites his psychic world, limiting it to one world shared with his two parents in which different object relationships can exist.
>
> (Britton 1993: 84)

This triangular space involves new experience and knowledge, including what, as adults, we take for granted, namely, 'the possibility of being a participant in a relationship and observed by a third person as well as being an observer of a relationship between two people' (ibid.). The depressive position is both provoked by this knowledge and establishes it. The triangle is only 'closed' if there is 'a recognition of a link joining the parents' (ibid.).

This emphasis on triangular space is an important supplement to the preoccupations of object relations theory, feminist ones included, with the two-person relationship. It leads to a stress on how critical is the internalisation of the parental *relationship* in the child's mind. Although Kleinians commonly imply that this will be the original parental relationship (which anyway will continue to exist in the parents' and child's minds), this analysis can be applied to other adults who create a triangular space by virtue of being in a sexual partnership with one or other parent.

The unique significance of the original father lies in three features, the first two of which are unavoidable. Firstly, in the child's mind, the father signifies as the joint creator, who therefore, by definition, precedes the child in relation to the mother. Secondly, the father exists anyway in the mother's mind, and therefore in the infant's mind through unconscious communications. The third feature depends on this father having been, and remaining, available; on the reality of his existence in the infant's 'prehistory'. From pre-Oedipal beginnings, a relationship can evolve with the Oedipal father (see Frosh on Kristeva, Chapter 3): no sudden threat, nothing new; only the child's gradually changing apprehension of its relationships.

The significance of a different sexual partner of the mother borrows some of the features of the original 'parental relationship'. What is equally significant about the father, or another partner of the mother, is that, at the same time as facing the child with the reality of triangular space, the child is coming to terms with a relationship from which, by definition, he or she is excluded. (This structure is also true in the case of lesbian parents.) How this adult sexual relationship signifies in terms of gender difference, how it impacts upon the child's achievement of gendered identification, will depend on the relationship of the parents, and theirs with other partners, that the child has internalised. The triangle can only be closed in the way that Britton is talking about if the infant has relationships to both parties, otherwise the third term (the 'father') will be experienced purely as a threat to the child's relationship to the mother and therefore only as an extension of the two-person relationship.

In other words, the quality of the parental relationship (to which the 'primal scene' symbolically refers), as well as that of the child with either parent, matters in the child's development. The implications of this are as profound for parents who stay together in a hostile, abusive or unequal relationship, or one devoid of respect and mutual recognition, as for single parents entering new relationships.

The achievement of triangular space is surely one of the difficulties of introducing a new partner into the family after a break-up between the parents. Several years and a different relationship on, I know that a new 'triangular space' is possible, premissed on dyadic relationships of mutual recognition. I do not believe its emotional importance is constricted to the period of Oedipal conflict, narrowly defined. In my daughter's case, as she moves into adolescence, she occupies triangular space in two households in which she has been able to come to terms with parental constellations (and sibling relationships).

Probably no psychoanalyst would disagree that the child's acceptance of an independent relationship between the parents, or between a parent and new partner, involves the acceptance of the parents' sexuality.[18] But it is not just about sex, nor even only about sex, gender and generation. The closure of the triangle is, in favourable circumstances, a secure foundation for coming to terms with the world beyond maternal dependence: 'the capacity to envisage a benign parental relationship influences the development of a space outside the self capable of being observed and thought about, which provides the basis for a belief in a secure and stable world' (Britton 1993: 84).[19] The implications of my argument about triangular space are that, in the case of an unlovable parent or a barely known 'step-parent', the closure of the triangle will be problematic.

An emphasis on the internalisation of the 'parental' relationship further displaces the idea of the father's authority as central to the child. It is replaced with an emphasis on the child experiencing, from those early prelinguistic beginnings, a relationship of which it is the observer that is outside. The parental relationship to be internalised by the infant may be based on defensive and depleting misrecognitions engendered by difference, or by projection and introjection of split parts, with little by way of the intervention of reality. In this case, the defensive entrenchment of sexual and gender difference will probably result. If, however, the parental relationship is characterised by care and mutual recognition (and not too much extraneous anxiety), the child finds out that, by foregoing the pre-Oedipal relationship with the mother, he or she is not foregoing love; that growing up need not be feared. Not only does the child not have to give up one or the other (and the parts of them that make up the child's self), but they do not have to vanquish one parent in order to have the other, or repudiate one to be the other. This knowledge depends on whether the sexualisation of infantile desires for recognition (desires which become sexualised with the recognition of the parental couple's sexual relationship) can be contained in the triangular space.

CONCLUSION

In this chapter, I have tried to outline the psychodynamics of two- and three-person relationships which can realistically exist between parents and children. These dynamics need not result in defensive – idealising or denigrating – relationships between men and women, nor rigid and depleted gendered subjectivities. Although the phantasies which characterise Oedipal dynamics are, in important respects, beyond the influence of actual parental care, this argument does have practical implications for mothers, fathers, other parental couples and carers. It first sees mothers (and other carers) as capable of having lives and relationships beyond their children, not just so that they are not prey to the infant's desire to maintain omnipotent control, but so that the infant can come to recognise the mother as a subject, who is desiring, and therefore capable of recognition. If no adult is capable of providing this recognition on a regular basis, the odds are stacked against that child achieving the autonomous subjectivity which, though misleadingly defined, is so prized in Oedipal theory.

More importantly, my framework involves not only a series of dyadic relationships, but triangular space, a space which is, by definition, sexualised in as much as it recognises, or resists recognising, both parents' sexuality. Given that a mother's desiring relationship to another is bound to be experienced by the child, if only unconsciously, issues of envy and loss arise. A third figure inevitably appears for the child and poses issues of external reality which are central to working through the depressive position. Whether this reality is more or less likely to be defended against by splitting or worked through to integration, whether it is likely to result in repudiation of the mother or renunciation of unrealistic desires to have or be her, will depend partly on the conditions which attach to the child's relationship with this third figure, as well as the mother. The parenting relationship which the infant and child internalises can provide a model of mutual recognition on which the child can build its own relationships with the adults in both parental positions, identifying with good internalised objects from both sources at the same time as acknowledging the reality that it cannot be both a girl and a boy (a mother and a father).

'Children need parents' seems an accurate slogan, if, as I have tried to show, the notion of a parent encompasses the following characteristics (which are relational accomplishments, rather than endowments of natural parents). Parenting involves being committed to the welfare of a child over time in a consistent manner; it involves accommodating the dramatically different requirements that a baby, later a child and an adolescent, needs in its object relations at different times in its development. It involves the capacity to relate to that child as separate from oneself and at the same time as dependent on that recognition. These are demanding requirements which, through parenting, can develop an adult's subjectivity (as in Parker's idea of 'maternal development'). Ideally, however, they would not be the responsibility of only one parent, or even two. I do not mean that children must have more than one to thrive, still less a mother and father in the same family. One parent may successfully bring up a child on her (or his) own. What that parent will need, if she or he is to be able to help the child acknowledge a reality beyond its early omnipotent phantasy of having that person all to itself, is a life beyond that child. That is one condition for mutual recognition, without which an autonomous subjectivity cannot grow, as Benjamin argues.

However, one further definition of a 'parent', in this analysis, is that it inevitably confronts the child with the idea of a threesome; that is, with the difficult realisation that it cannot have the mother (later also father) all to itself. This returns me to the significance of the maternal bed. To the extent that it is shared with a sexual partner,[20] the bed will come to symbolise, not simply the mother's sexuality, but the mother's desires for one who is not her child; one who has privileges from which the child is excluded. If the bed has always been the parental bed, the way the child gradually experiences and comes to know this reality will be different from if the child is displaced or excluded from these privileges by an unfamiliar person (of whatever sex). If the mother has a sexual partner, it will be made sense of in terms of all the child's pressing issues (depending on the child's age as to how they are made sense of): their own vulnerable self and gendered subjectivity, their dependency, their envy, their sexuality, their rivalrousness.

What is crucial is not whether this newcomer is a paternal figure (in the sense that he or she can exercise authority and privilege) but the quality of their relationship to the mother and, gradually, to the child or children. Can they recognise the child and be guided into finding an appropriate space, flexible with the developing relationship? (Parker's ambivalence and capacity to think would apply here, as would Frosh's father's 'presence, calm, and thoughtful love'.) Can they contain the child's rivalrous claims for the mother, neither giving up their own existence in the threesome nor fighting back? Can they contain their own rivalrousness and envy for the child's privileged position (for the adult is not the only one with privileges)? Can they enable the closure of the Oedipal triangle? If not, the presence of this newcomer will exacerbate the fears and phantasies that abound under the conditions of a breakdown of the parental relationship (as I described at the beginning of the chapter) and be an anxiety-provoking circumstance which many children would not survive well.

However, if these conditions are available to the child, the maternal bed can become a benign space signifying, not only the sexual character of generational difference but a pleasurable reality to which the child of either sex can aspire in the future. Under such good-enough conditions, the child will have the added resource not only of a (another) good-enough parent, but of the experience of a good-enough adult relationship which can be internalised, as well as a reassuring, rather than threatening, developmental space for the present. The quality of this adult relationship is of crucial importance to the development of gendered subjectivity. It is also a site of change.

ACKNOWLEDGEMENTS

Thanks to Tony Jefferson and Cathy Urwin for helping me through some difficult developments of these ideas. Thanks and admiration go to my daughter for agreeing to figure in this chapter, for adding some perceptive comments and for justifying my confidence in the ideas I have developed here.

NOTES

1 The family of three is relatively unusual, except for the first few years of the first child's life. However, it has come to encapsulate the Oedipal dynamics that are central to a psychoanalytic understanding of sexual and gender relations. Psychoanalysis has under-theorised the role of siblings in Oedipal conflicts.
2 In Nini Herman's autobiography (1988), this separation of the children from adult life is insightfully described as she details her childhood in pre-war Berlin. See also Ronald Fraser's autobiography (1984).
3 For example:

> For it was the forced, close, daily contact between the mother (situated in the home without a career) and her child – a contact now divorced from the labor within the preindustrial home in which children always engaged – that elicited the Oedipal neuroses Freud theorized.
>
> (Kaplan 1992: 27)

4 David Jackson, in an autobiographical exploration of his early gendered development, reconstructs one night, soon after his father's homecoming after the war, when he started to have nightmares:

> He slowly inched the door open to his parents' bedroom. He stopped still for a moment listening anxiously to his mother's breathing. It was as if there were cords that attached him to the soft rise and fall of her breathing ... With held breath the boy edged himself under the sheet and eiderdown, on his mother's side of the bed closest to the door. He snuggled into her safe, warm thigh ... The boy slid his left arm under

the pillow and nuzzled his nose down deeply into the warm, pillow scent of his mother's hair. He was the right size again. He could go to sleep here and forget his fear.

(Jackson 1990: 74–5)

5 In the stories of disturbed childhoods which frequently accompany press reports of newsworthy criminals, the succession of boyfriends who pass through the home – men who may rapidly assume paternal rights over the child – is frequently recorded but rarely analysed. For example, see Smith (1995).

6 See Collier (1996) for a detailed deconstruction of the new father discourse. Social work has had to reflect on this question when decisions must be made whether to leave a child with a mother or to take the child into care, but expectations of the father have been very different.

7 As Benjamin (1990a: 278) points out, Lasch 'drew heavily on the more sophisticated arguments of the Frankfurt school' which used the basic Freudian notion of a loss of autonomy in the adult character if declining paternal authority led to an inadequate Oedipal resolution. See also Benjamin 1978, 1981.

8 Despite Oedipal theory which implies the contrary, psychoanalytic writers as well as developmental psychologists (for example, Stern 1985) have convincingly documented the child's own capacity to become autonomous from adult carers, over time. For example, according to Britton, the achievement of the depressive position 'arises inevitably and naturally in infancy as a consequence of the developing capacities of the child: to perceive, to recognise, to remember, to locate or to anticipate experience' (Britton 1992: 38). Winnicott, for all the feminist criticism he has received, depicted the gradual moves of the infant away from the mother through his concepts of 'transitional space' and 'play' and 'making good use of the object' (see, for example, First 1988, 1994).

9 The presence or absence of a new sexual partner will have effects, but even if there is not currently a sexual partner, there has got to have been one – the child's father. This is why the relationship to the father in the mother's mind is influential. See pp. 69–72.

10 In Freudian theory this recognition turns into an account which assumes the inextricability of the child's experience of their masculinity or femininity on the one hand and their sexual object choice on the other. It is this connectedness which makes most contemporary orthodox psychoanalysis so obdurate on the question of homosexuality, still often seeing it as a 'perversion'.

11 According to Steiner, the jealousy aroused frequently involves the use of projective identification that is identifying with one or other of the parents and thus participating in the parents' intercourse (Steiner 1993: 97).

12 Early infancy, for Klein, is characterised by splitting defences which protect the 'good breast' (or other good object) from the 'bad breast', so that the mother as the source of both satisfaction and frustration cannot be recognised as one object. This splitting of good and bad is

paradigmatic of the paranoid-schizoid position (to which we all commonly resort to defend against anxiety). The move to the depressive position involves the difficult recognition of good and bad coming from the same source, and with this capacity to relate to others as integrated and separate comes the capacity to experience an integrated, separate self. Klein's account of the move from the paranoid-schizoid to depressive position is arguably as important for understanding the origins of subjectivity as Freud's Oedipus.

13 Working through the depressive position is not a once-for-all achievement, but one which will be repeated 'with each new addition to experience or knowledge' (Britton 1992: 38).

14 '[T]hings which are and always have been hostile to us, we simply deny' (Ferenczi 1926/1980: 371, quoted in Parker 1995: 7).

15 Prehistoric in the sense of a father who pre-exists memory and language in the child's experience.

16 'Real' here does not mean 'natural', but real as opposed to in phantasy.

17 Since writing this chapter, Benjamin's newest work has appeared, which, while retaining an emphasis on dyadic relationships (notably including one with the '*rapprochement*' father), gestures to a later triangle:

> What I wish to underscore is the importance of a second adult, not necessarily a male or a father, with whom the child can form a second dyad. The key feature of this person, or position, is not yet that he or she loves the mother and seals the triangle, but that he or she creates the second vector which points outward and on which the triangle can be formed.
>
> (Benjamin 1995b: 57)

This is closely consistent with my directions in this chapter.

18 For Money-Kyrle, it is one of three primal 'facts of life' which present such difficulties for children that they colour all adult development. These are 'the recognition of the breast as a supremely good object, the recognition of the parents' intercourse as a supremely creative act, and the recognition of the inevitability of time and ultimately death' (1971: 443, quoted in Steiner 1993: 95). Coming to terms with the first involves acknowledging that there is an outside source of satisfaction, which is not therefore under the control of the infant. This is what Chasseguet-Smirgel calls the 'narcissistic wound', which links to Benjamin's outside source of recognition, because both are about renouncing omnipotence. It therefore involves a self–other distinction, as well as a good–bad one, but it is basically two-person. This is the essence of working through the depressive position. The second 'fact of life', the parents' intercourse, involves the intrusion of a third object into the baby–mother relationship.

19 See Parker, Chapter 2, who argues that the capacity to think by the mother can provide the containing space for the child. The two accounts are not mutually exclusive.

20 Even if not shared with a sexual partner, at some point this will still be experienced through a sexual frame, for example, as the child's success in keeping potential sexual partners at bay.

REFERENCES

Barrett, M. and McIntosh, M. (1982) *The Anti-social Family*, London: Verso.

Bassin, D., Honey M. and Kaplan Mahrer, M. (eds) (1994) *Representations of Motherhood*, New Haven: Yale University Press.

Benjamin, J. (1978) 'Authority and the Family Revisited', *New German Critique*, 13: 52–3.

—— (1981) 'The Oedipal Riddle: Authority and the New Narcissism', in J. Diggins and M. Kamin (eds) *The Problem of Authority in America*, Philadelphia: Temple.

—— (1984) 'Master and Slave: The Fantasy of Erotic Domination', in A. Snitow, C. Standell and S. Thompson (eds) *Desire: The Politics of Sexuality*, London: Virago.

—— (1990a) *The Bonds of Love*, London: Virago.

—— (1990b) 'An Outline of Inter-subjectivity: The Development of Recognition', *Psychoanalytic Psychology*, 7, supplement: 33–46.

—— (1994) 'The Omnipotent Mother: A Psychoanalytic Study of Fantasy and Reality', in D. Bassin, M. Honey and M. Mahrer Kaplan (eds) *Representations of Motherhood*, New Haven and London: Yale University Press, Chapter 7: 129–46.

—— (1995a) 'Sameness and Difference: Towards an "Over-inclusive" Theory of Gender Development', in A. Elliott and S. Frosh (eds) *Psychoanalysis in Contexts: Paths between Theory and Modern Culture*, London: Routledge, Chapter 6: 106–22.

—— (1995b) *Like Subjects, Love Objects: Essays on Recognition and Sexual Difference*, New Haven and London: Yale University Press.

Breen, D. (ed.) (1993) *The Gender Conundrum*, London: Routledge.

Britton, R. (1992) 'The Oedipus Situation and the Depressive Position', in R. Anderson (ed.) *Clinical Lectures on Klein and Bion*, London: Routledge, Chapter 3: 34–45.

—— (1993) 'The Missing Link: Parental Sexuality in the Oedipus Complex', in D. Breen (ed.) *The Gender Conundrum*, London: Routledge, Chapter 3: 82–4.

Collier, R. (1996) ' "Coming Together?": Post-heterosexuality, Masculine Crisis and the New Men's Movement', *Feminist Legal Studies*, 4(1): 3–48.

Dally, A. (1982) *Inventing Motherhood: The Consequences of an Ideal*, London: Burnett Books.

First, E. (1988) 'The Leaving Game: I'll Play You and You'll Play Me', in A. Slade and D. Wolfe (eds) *Models of Meaning: Clinical and Developmental Approaches to Symbolic Play*, New York: Oxford University Press: 132–60.

—— (1994) 'Mothering, Hate and Winnicott', in D. Bassin *et al.* (eds) *Representations of Motherhood*, New Haven: Yale University Press, Chapter 8: 147–61.

Fraser, R. (1984) *In Search of a Past: The Manor House, Ammersfield, 1933–1945*, London: Verso.

Greenson, R. R. (1993) 'Disidentifying from Mother: Its Special Importance for the Boy', in D. Breen (ed.) *The Gender Conundrum*, London: Routledge: 258–64.

Herman, N. (1988) *My Kleinian Home: A Journey through Four Psychotherapies*, London: Free Association Books.

Hollway, W. (1996) 'Recognition and Heterosexual Desire', in D. Richardson (ed.) *Theorizing Heterosexuality: Telling it Straight*, Milton Keynes: Open University Press: 91–108.

Jackson, D. (1990) *Unmasking Masculinity: A Critical Autobiography*, London: Unwin Hyman.

Kaplan, E. Ann (1992) *Motherhood and Representation*, London: Routledge.

Klein, M. (1933) 'The Early Development of Conscience in the Child', in M. Klein *Love, Guilt and Reparation and Other Works, 1921–1945*, Vol. 1. of *The Writings of Melanie Klein* (eds) R. E. Money-Kyrle, B. Joseph, E. O'Shaughnessy and H. Segal, London: Hogarth Press (1975) and London: Virago (1994).

—— (1945) 'The Oedipus Complex in the Light of Early Anxieties', in *Love, Guilt and Reparation and Other Works 1921–1945*.

Lasch, C. (1977) *Haven in a Heartless World*, New York: Basic Books.

Lévi-Strauss, C. (1969) *Totemism*, Harmondsworth: Penguin.

McDougall, J. (1993) 'The Dead Father: On Early Psychic Trauma and its Relation to Disturbance in Sexual Identity and in Creative Activity', in D. Breen (ed.) *The Gender Conundrum*, London: Routledge, Chapter 11: 233–57.

Mens-Verhulst J., Schreurs, K. and Woertman, L. (eds) (1993) *Daughtering and Mothering: Female Subjectivity Reanalysed*, London: Routledge.

Mitchell, J. (1974) *Psychoanalysis and Feminism*, Harmondsworth: Penguin.

Parker, R. (1995) *Torn in Two: The Experience of Maternal Ambivalence*, London: Virago.

Sayers, J. (1995) 'Consuming Male Fantasy: Feminist Psychoanalysis Retold', in A. Elliot and S. Frosh (eds) *Psychoanalysis in Contexts: Paths between Theory and Modern Culture*, London: Routledge, Chapter 7: 123–41.

Smith, D. J. (1995) *The Sleep of Reason: The James Bulger Case*, London: Arrow.

Steiner, J. (1993) *Psychic Retreats*, London: Routledge.

Stern, D. (1985) *The Interpersonal World of the Infant*, New York: Basic Books.

Temperley, J. (1993) 'Is the Oedipus Complex Bad News for Women?', *Free Associations*, 4(2) (No. 30): 265–75.

Thurer, S. L. (1994) *The Myths of Motherhood: How Culture Reinvents the Good Mother*, Boston: Houghton Mifflin.

Chapter 5

Mothers and daughters within a changing world

Sheila Ernst

As an adolescent I recoiled when told that I was like my mother; many years later I acknowledged some of our similarities with pride. That mothers' and daughters' shared anatomy and gender poses daughters with a unique developmental task is more than an anatomical truism. Almost all contemporary cultures conflate femininity and maternity and then idealise and denigrate both. Mothers bear and still primarily care for children, within a framework which, at present, is in a state of major transition. Within the traditional framework, sons are expected to disidentify with their primary love-object, their mother, in order to identify themselves with their fathers; daughters need to find a way of establishing themselves as people who have some kind of mastery (*sic*) over their environment, separate from mother, and yet identify with mother as a woman. Mothers inevitably internalise society's ambivalence about maternity and this may particularly affect their mothering of daughters (women and mothers-to-be), both in early provision for the infant and in providing the environment within which the capacity to 'play', to be 'creative' and to become a person in her own right, will be formed. Psychoanalysis provides a way of thinking about the implications of these social transitions.

RECENT FEMINIST THINKING ABOUT THE RELATIONSHIP BETWEEN MOTHER AND DAUGHTER

The debate about the nature of femininity began almost as soon as women became psychoanalysts. It raged in the 1920s and 1930s and then quietened down until feminists became interested in psychoanalysis again in the early 1970s (see Maguire 1995: Chapter 1).

They wanted to understand how women's own psychology might be contributing to their social oppression. Mitchell's famous book of the period, *Psychoanalysis and Feminism* (1974), presented an understanding of men's and women's development within patriarchy. While Mitchell argued that she was offering an account of why women were the way they were, the book was also seen as reactionary, both in its apparent acceptance of the categories of patriarchy and its implication that the power of the unconscious made change extremely difficult.

Meanwhile, other feminists, often clinicians, turned to object relations theory within psychoanalysis, which placed the mother–infant relationship at the centre of psychological development. Their fresh emphasis was on the importance of gender difference and its social origins and on the mother–daughter relationship as the site of the internalisation of women's oppression. This viewpoint developed on both sides of the Atlantic; in the USA starting with Chodorow (1978), (who at that time was not a clinician but a sociologist), and in Britain at the Women's Therapy Centre (Eichenbaum and Orbach 1982). I see my own work as being part of this tradition (Ernst 1987) and am engaged in the relevant critical debates and developments which are raised in different chapters of this book (see, for example, Featherstone, Chapters 1 and 11).

Three points concern us here. First, is the way in which in writing about *the* mother–daughter relationship can seem to deny both social and cultural differences and the fact that each mother–daughter pair is unique. Second, there is a tendency to move from a position where the boy's development is seen as the norm, to an equally problematic position of 'the valorization of maternity and female relatedness within contemporary feminist discourses' (Flax 1993: 60). A third and related problem is that it may appear to reinforce the binding quality of the mother–daughter dyad as if no 'third' person were significantly involved in the daughter's development. In trying to critique both the original Freudian position that the girl must and does transfer her attachment from mother to father, and the feminist position pointing out the inevitability of this move within patriarchy, the significance of both the father and/ or other key figures in the girl's development may be overlooked.

Each of these problems requires holding a tension between two polarities and valuing the creativity of that tension. In writing about gender as a category one must be aware of how this reifies the very stereotypes one wishes to challenge (Frosh 1994). My own clinical experience, particularly with the diversity of class, culture and race at the Women's Therapy Centre amongst clients and staff, made me aware of the value of both generalising and particularising about work with women.

Psychoanalytic thinking well understands that the tendency to split between two polarities rather than hold the tension between them arises from infants' earliest need to separate out the good mother/breast from the withholding or depriving aspects of their experience. The difference between men and women has been construed in a similar defensive fashion with, as Dinnerstein (1976) has pointed out, the aim of preserving the fantasy that men can still be infants in relation to women as carers and that women stay infants in relation to men who deal with the outside world and protect them from it. The power of this defensive fantasy is reflected in its lack of correspondence to the actual needs of men and women within a post-industrial society.

When feminists began to rewrite the story of a child's development so that it no longer suggested that the boy's development was the norm from which the girl deviated, perhaps some were unconsciously pulled back into the gender split Dinnerstein described, and so found themselves almost idealising the feminine way. Gilligan and Rogers argue that there has been a paradigm shift as 'a psychology premised on a view of human life as lived ultimately in separation has given way to a psychology that rests on a view of human life as lived essentially in relationship' (1993: 125).

The disturbing aspect of this approach is that it suggests that hearing girls' voices speaking to their mothers will have a socially transformative power. To listen to women's voices can redress the balance and draw attention to the negativity of stereotypical gender identity which splits women who 'relate' from men who are 'autonomous' and 'independent'. However, it implies that there is nothing wrong with the splitting in itself but rather with society's mistaken evaluation. The underlying unconscious conflicts within both men and women are once again denied. Much of this book is concerned with the ways in which this splitting and the consequent idealisation and denigration of mothers and fathers reduces our human experience as children, parents and people.

Clinical and theoretical work, often from a feminist perspective, has returned to the importance of further investigating the dissociated cross-gender elements in both men and women, which Winnicott (1971b) described as being fundamentally involved in the formation of the self. Benjamin (1988) is a good example of a feminist writing from a psychoanalytic perspective who sets out to explore the problematic of domination and submission in relationships between men and women, making explicit the complementarity of the subject and the object. Thus, the task becomes not the valorising of the feminine but the understanding of the unconscious roots of apparent gender polarity.

Clinical writing, which develops this tendency, argues that it is the therapist's task to maintain an awareness of potential bisexuality and the ways in which gender stereotyping can make the therapist blind to what is actually happening both within the patient and in the counter-transference.

Elliott (1987) suggests that the therapy group evokes the group members' bisexuality, making it an environment within which men can become aware of their more stereotypically feminine parts and women can discover their masculine elements, assuming the group conductor does not allow group members simply to reinforce their defences against seeing these hidden parts. A women-only therapy group can also be used to show how aspects of women's personalities which might usually be projected onto men may still emerge in the group; thus one woman may be seen in the group as silent and withholding her emotions, while another may be experienced as dominating and bullying. This counteracts fantasies of the idyllic, open and communicative all-women setting, showing that stereotypically masculine aspects are often present. (Chapter 10 will look in detail at the specific contribution which group-analytic therapy can make.)

Welldon (1988) argues that women, with less access to traditionally masculine forms of power, turn their aggression and need to control onto the sites of their own bodies and their children. Like Elliott, she emphasises the ways in which our expectations dictate what we see; thus, we have difficulty in acknowledging that women can abuse/sexually abuse their children (see Featherstone, Chapter 11) or in seeing the violence involved in some traditionally feminine behaviour.

Therapy can provide a site for the exploration of such socially significant issues as how a single female parent can provide feminine and masculine aspects of care or how two women can relate intimately without the relationship involving a denial of difference. This necessitates developing a gendered view of transference and counter-transference. Maguire (1995) implies that the practising clinician must recognise that both mother and father appear in the therapy relationship, even when the two participants are both women, thus avoiding an exclusive focus on the mother within the daughter's therapy. The daughter need no longer be the mother's sole responsibility. Conlon (1991) and Prodgers (1990) remind the group conductor not to assume that all discussion about power in the therapy group is connected to masculinity. They both emphasise that maternal projections onto the conductor may derive from fantasies about the very powerful and potentially destructive mother as well as the soft maternal presence.

These developments in the thinking about gender in individual and group therapy have implications for thinking about the relationships between mothers and their daughters.

RELATIONSHIPS BETWEEN MOTHER AND DAUGHTER

The infant's developing identity can most usefully be understood as part of a relationship in which, on the one hand, there is a need for relating, mutuality and recognition and, on the other, a need to negotiate a series of separations.

To understand the way in which this has happened for any individual woman, it is crucial to seek out the ways in which the mother (I shall use the term 'mother' in this context to refer to any female primary carer) experiences her daughter as being the *same* as her. This will affect the mother both because she will perhaps identify with her daughter and also because she will project onto her daughter (either directly or by trying to negate them) those social images of a woman which she herself has internalised. The mother and her daughter may well struggle with this but they will be affected by it, just as a black mother and daughter are specifically affected by white society's racist images of black women (see, for an example, Mama 1995: 132–3). How, precisely, this works will be different from one individual to the next.

Modifying Winnicott's model of the developing relationship between mother and infant to apply it specifically to the girl child (see Ernst 1987), we see how the mother may unconsciously be particularly connected to her infant daughter's experience. The mother's identification with her daughter may make it harder to achieve her wish to meet her daughter's every need, in this way developing what Winnicott terms a 'holding environment' in which there is some continuity between the environment of the womb and the infant's first experience in the world. As the mother mirrors her infant daughter's gaze, she may find it difficult to keep her own needs and feelings to herself, thus failing to protect her daughter from inappropriate expressions of her own feelings. If the sameness of mother and daughter affects the mother's capacity to protect her daughter from impingement, then the daughter may begin to develop what Winnicott termed a 'false self' to protect her incipient self from intrusion.

This may reduce both mother's and daughter's ability to enter into the arena of 'creative playing' (where the mother can make a safe space for her daughter to try things out and learn through her own experience). The mother herself needs to have an internalised trust in the possibility of experiencing life in this way, which can come only from her own sense of selfhood. This, Winnicott suggests, stems from the infant's learning that she/he can interact with others rather than experiencing them either as being controlled or controlling. Winnicott describes how the child discovers that even if she/he hates the object (mother), the object can survive. Through seeing the object's survival the child realises that she/he too is a separate being: the object can be 'used' (Winnicott 1971a). In the relationship between mother and daughter, the confluence of cultural context and the sameness of gender means that the mother may find it particularly difficult to engage in this vital struggle with her daughter. She herself may have a weak sense of her own capacity to 'use' an object; moreover, her identification with her daughter may make it difficult to stay in her position as the object to be struggled with.

The girl's genital anxieties (which are quite different from the boy's) may further affect and influence what we can already see is a complex and multi-determined process. An American feminist psychoanalyst, Bernstein (1993) argues that the girl's genital anxieties influence the ways in which she attempts to establish her mastery, firstly in relation to her body and then in relation to others in the world. She points out that the girl does not have the same access to her genitals as the boy does, making it difficult for her to have a mental representation of a part of her body which nevertheless has intense sensations. She cannot touch it and manipulate it in the desexualised way that the boy can his penis, so she has no means of gaining mastery of this part of her body without sexual fantasies being involved. Perhaps most importantly her genital area is a bodily opening over which there is little control, unlike the mouth and the anus.

Without seeing anatomy as destiny, Bernstein argues that these differences impact upon the girl's development so that when she is striving for increased mastery over the world, she may regress, for instance to a preoccupation with anal mastery or, in adolescence, to the pseudo-mastery of oral control involved in anorexia or bulimia, to reassure herself that she can control her orifices.

Suffering a period of confusion, the girl will turn to both mother and father, making complex and contradictory demands to help her establish her sense of herself. Her mother will need to be able to accept the girl's genital anxieties and validate the girl's sexuality, although both may evoke the mother's own complex and even self-denigratory feelings. The mother may be anxious about the girl's sexual feelings towards her which, as part of a subtle homophobia, may be denied. The mother needs to show her daughter that she can accept and stand up to her aggression. How mother and daughter negotiate their relationship will depend on a complex interaction between the internal object world of each woman (particularly the degree to which the mother is able to contain her own anxieties) and their social and relational context.

The 'father' is *symbolically* present in the patriarchal social context within which the daughter is developing. The actual father (and other significant people) may play an important part, both in facilitating the re-negotiation between mother and daughter and as someone for the daughter to identify with (as the boy uses his father). Closeness with his daughter may evoke sexual feelings and/or his repressed feelings for his mother. Sometimes the father may deal with this by encouraging his daughter's identification while denigrating women, thus making the daughter feel that she can have certain stereotypically masculine attributes only if she disidentifies with her mother.

For many of the women whom I see and hear about, in both group and individual therapy, the relationship with mother has not been successfully negotiated at the early stage of development. In adolescence the child revisits, and may work through, infantile conflicts as part of her growing up (Apter 1990). Pines (1993) suggests that it is characteristic of the woman's life-cycle that at each stage she may rework early conflicts. For example, at adolescence, a daughter struggling to be like her mother and yet have confidence in her capacity to be somebody apart from mother may substitute control over what enters her body through her mouth, i.e., anorexia, for attempting to take some control outside of herself. She appears to be totally rejecting mother's food. Yet, unconsciously, she may be deeply connected to her mother and unable to find a way of revealing and working through the conflict to a point of tolerable ambivalence. For this to happen the mother also needs to recognise and acknowledge her own ambivalence (see Parker, Chapter 2).

In therapy the woman/daughter often begins to recognise her similarities to her mother as she begins to feel more aware of her own internal world. She may become more aware of herself responding as her mother would have done, as Zoe Heller, nearing 30, describes what she sees in the mirror, 'tracing the faint lines that wind away from the corners of my eyes, like tributary rivers on a map. I am, I realise, the best memento I have of her' (1995: 12).

REFERENCES

Apter, T. (1990) *Altered Loves*, Hemel Hempstead: Harvester Wheatsheaf.
Benjamin, J. (1988) *Bonds of Love*, New York: Pantheon.
Bernstein, D. (1993) *Female Identity Conflict in Clinical Practice*, New York: Aronson.
Chodorow, N. (1978) *The Reproduction of Mothering*, Berkeley: University of California Press.
Conlon, I. (1991) 'Effect of Gender on the Role of Female Group Conductor', *Group Analysis*, 24(2): 187–200.
Dinnerstein, D. (1976) *The Mermaid and the Minotaur: Sexual Arrangements and Human Malaise*, New York: Harper & Row.
Eichenbaum, L. and Orbach, S. (1982) *Understanding Women*, New York: Basic Books.
Elliott, B. (1987) 'Gender-identity in Group-analytic Psychotherapy', *Group Analysis*, 19(3): 195–206.
Ernst, S. (1987) 'Can a Daughter be a Woman?', in S. Ernst and M. Maguire (eds) *Living with the Sphinx: Papers from the Women's Therapy Centre*, London: Women's Press.
Flax, J. (1993) *Disputed Subjects: Essays on Psychoanalysis, Politics and Philosophy*, New York: Routledge.
Frosh, S. (1994) *Sexual Difference: Masculinity and Psychoanalysis*, London: Routledge.
Gilligan, C. and Rogers, A. (1993) 'Reframing Daughtering and Mothering: A Paradigm Shift in Psychology', in J. van Mens-Verhulst, K. Schreurs and L. Woertman (eds) *Daughtering and Mothering*, London: Routledge.
Heller, Z. (1995) 'Caroline Carter: 1931–1990', in J. Goldsworthy (ed.) *Mothers by Daughters*, London: Virago.

Maguire, M. (1995) *Men, Women, Passion, Power. Gender Issues in Psychotherapy*, London: Routledge.

Mama, A. (1995) *Beyond the Masks*, London: Routledge.

Mitchell, J. (1974) *Psychoanalysis and Feminism*, London: Allen Lane.

Pines, D. (1993) *A Woman's Unconscious Use of her Body*, London: Virago.

Prodgers, A. (1990) 'The Dual Nature of the Group as Mother: The Uroboric Container', *Group Analysis*, 23(1): 17–30.

Welldon, E. (1988) *Mother, Madonna, Whore*, London: Free Association Books.

Winnicott, D.W. (1971a) 'The Use of an Object and Relating through Identification', in D.W. Winnicott *Playing and Reality*, London: Tavistock.

—— (1971b) 'Creativity and its Origins', in D.W. Winnicott *Playing and Reality*, London: Tavistock.

Chapter 6

Susie Orbach talking to Wendy Hollway about mothers, parenting, gender development and therapy

IDENTIFICATION BETWEEN MOTHER AND CHILD

Susie Orbach starts by outlining what she sees as the core problem in the mother–daughter relationship: that of the unconscious identifications which make it difficult for both mother and daughter to separate, that is, to know the difference between their own feelings and each other's and therefore to be able to experience clearly who they are. This has been and remains an important theme in Susie's work, and in her joint work with Luise Eichenbaum.

SO It is a continual conflict that comes up: that women, on the one hand, will describe wanting to be this good mother. They know they should only be good enough, that you don't have to be perfect. But there's still a notion of being perfect. On the other hand, how do they manage that when they feel so entwined with their children's lives?

WH How do women express this being entwined? Is it something that they diagnose in themselves in their own terms?

SO Oh yes, I think mothers will often say: 'when I had my daughter I just thought I was looking at myself, I want my daughter to have everything I didn't have. I don't want her to have the unhappy childhood I had.' I don't think they have any difficulty in making the conscious links of identification. It is the repercussions of those identifications and their unconscious elaborations that are problematic. I think if I were to boil down what they experience, it would be that they don't know how to tolerate their children's feelings. They often feel incapable of allowing their children their own emotional reactions. Mothers can be ashamed about their own incapacity to do that. Or they're annoyed about their children's rebellion. You can see it in terms of the problem of recognising this person as a separate little person.

WH   So if we look at that in terms of identification, here is this person with whom you identify closely, expressing emotions which you would feel afraid of or anxious about in yourself and you have to silence them wherever they come up, in yourself or your daughter or your son, I'd say.

SO   Well, you may allow certain things – unconsciously you may assign those to another gender, so making them permissible, but they may not be permissible in your daughter. You can have the obverse, where you absolutely encourage your daughter's rage because it's something that you can't own for yourself. And they can happen in the same relationship; in other words, I think the difficulty is in the inconsistency. It's that at one moment, as the mother, you can't bear your daughter's unhappiness because you can't bear the despair you feel yourself, right. So one moment the mother can really empathise and help her daughter to handle the range of feelings. And then another time her daughter tries to express it, she'll feel inside and maybe say 'grow up, don't be ridiculous'. Now in one of those instances she's having to curb what she's finding unacceptable, and in the other she's allowed some space for it. And that is part of the confusion. Sometimes you can hear the same thing from the mother talking about her own relationship with her mum. Sometimes it's OK to have certain feelings and sometimes it isn't. That is one of the most confusing things in the mother–daughter relationship.

SOCIAL SUPPORTS FOR WHAT PARENTS AND CHILDREN NEED

Applying feminist psychoanalysis to the questions of socialised child care which were prominent in Britain in the 1970s, our discussion emphasises the quality of emotional care provided in nurseries. In this sense, any child needs a good-enough nursery just as it needs a good-enough mother or a good-enough father – especially if the latter two are in short supply. So, when it comes to child care, although we start with the need to provide socialised child care on behalf of parents – in practice, mothers in particular – our emphasis is on what children need. Practically speaking, most mothers will avoid sending their children to nursery if the quality of emotional care is poor.

WH   We've agreed on the importance of there being more than one parent around, which I think is for the benefit of the children and the parents, and that this is politically difficult to reconcile with the attack on lone mothers at present.

SO   Well, I suppose you could make that a political response by thinking that it's not that we should be attacking lone mothers, or even the absent fathers, but we ought to be thinking about what the children require and what kind of support system can make it possible for them to grow up feeling OK about themselves. We ought not to keep relinquishing ground and letting the Right run the debate on this.

WH   And when you say the Right, you're also talking about conventional psychoanalysis?

SO   Exactly.

WH   For example, the way that Christopher Lasch used psychoanalysis in the American debate on the family?

SO   Exactly.

WH   So it's about forms of support for lone mothers.

SO   Absolutely, and a life for them. That's two points, isn't it? It's what feminism has understood, what contemporary gender-conscious psychoanalysis has understood, about women needing to be able to develop their own subjectivity and that mothering doesn't stop that desire or need. So it's both about providing single mothers with another identity as well as mothering – as well as providing something else for the kids, so that these children need not be isolated with their mothers.

WH   That's one example of the way that something slipped out of the debate which was always there in the 1970s, which is socialised child care. I mean partly because it feels so pessimistic now, doesn't it? It's become, not about making it better, but about stopping it getting worse.

SO Yes. The nursery debate doesn't actually include the content of what should be going on in those nurseries, about how to address the emotional needs of children (unless of course it is how to manage the 'difficult' children). It's been about physical care and now it's about extending the national curriculum and what they have to have achieved by the age of 4.

WH What should be included in the emotional needs to be taken care of in socialised child-care provision?

SO It would be the capacity of the carers to tolerate the range of children's emotional responses, so that children grow up with a much greater vocabulary than they would if they were stuck with one parent, whether the parent is in a heterosexual union or a single mother at home, or whatever. It's about providing recognition for areas that may be underdeveloped emotionally in children. It's providing words for emotional states in a matter-of-fact way. It's acknowledging problematic feelings, mixed emotions, as well as the positive feelings children have. It means making it safe for them to have a different emotional repertoire than they are able to have in their primary relationship.

WH And for that, the carers need to be there on a fairly continuous basis, don't they? So that there isn't a sort of merry-go-round of new carers?

SO Absolutely. That is what psychoanalysis can contribute. We know about the cost of things going wrong. We know the kinds of things that help things go right: continuity of care, a capacity to tolerate a wide range of emotions, not be frightened of intimacy, the capacity for attachment – all of those things make children's lives very, very different.

WH There's no debate in social policy which is informed by this?

SO I think there's attachment theory coming in now to Labour Party thinking, but not significantly. And I think most feminist debate about nursery education is still gender-based – you know, boys and girls and trains and dolls – as opposed to helping boys to take responsibility for their own emotional lives, and girls for theirs instead of everybody else's. I don't think the general analysis has come in at the right level.

WH   It's still anti-sexist socialisation training...

SO   Which does have some importance, but I don't think it's the cutting edge of what makes boys boys, or what makes boys' lives so difficult for them, or what makes girls' lives so difficult for them.

WH   Yes, it assumes that education can change their behaviour at a rational level, rather than engaging with children's emotional life.

MEDIATION PROVISION FOR SEPARATING PARENTS

More and more infants and children are faced at some point with the distress of their parents' separation. Law reform concerning divorce under the Conservative government has prioritised the preservation of the family unit irrespective of the quality of emotional relations in that unit. The mediation provisions have been fought for on the grounds that the quality of the parental relationship during and after divorce will make a significant difference in children's ability to acknowledge and come to terms with their parents' separation without recourse to the kind of rigid defences which will damage their relations to others and exacerbate their unhappiness. This, according to Susie Orbach, is another example of the way that psychodynamic understanding can influence social policy and indeed make it more rational.

SO   There's a failure of the public conversation to recognise the difficulties that divorce brings. What we've got now is the ideology that divorce is bad. And appalling research showing that children whose parents stay together do better. I just don't buy that research at all. But we've got no kind of commitment to talking about how, when parents get on very badly and there is a separation, that process can be managed: what those parents require so that they can continue to parent and to be grown ups. So, yes, it is a failure of policy. But I don't think that would be a difficult policy to put in place. I think the mediation provisions in the Family Law Bill are really important. A lot of us fought very hard for that. We know that most of the time parents play out their stuff with their children. It doesn't take an awful lot to make that happen in a different kind of way.

WH   So that's a practical example of ways in which psychodynamic knowledge, broadly understood, has fed into policy – into legislation in that example.

SO   Absolutely, and I think – and maybe this is the reformist in me – that psychoanalysis is wonderful at explaining the irrational and the subversive and the thing that doesn't fit, and all the madnesses. But out of that understanding you can get a much more rational policy. It doesn't defy rationality at the end of the day; it could underpin a rational policy.

MOTHERING OR PARENTING?

Susie Orbach read most of the book chapters (those that were ready at the time) and in our discussion, she picked up what seems to be politically one of the most paradoxical issues in feminist debates on mothering in Britain at the moment: the significance of the mother as her child's primary object.

SO   I do think there's a real problem. It's that the gains of feminism have been quite limited and theres' normative stuff around, about gender, about what mothers' roles are and what fathers' roles are, whereas twenty years ago these ideas were being contested. It's as though we accept that what needs to happen in the mother–child relationship is what needs to happen there, as opposed to what needs to happen in a parenting relationship. I think there is the elevation of the mother as the primary object. I think that in these essays what's come through is the significance of the mother. Now I don't want to undermine that significance. But in feminist scholarship we problematised the mother–daughter relationship, and we talked for a decade or so about why certain kinds of things happened in individual relationships and why they could be said to be social phenomena. It had to do with what gets transmitted between mother and daughter. But it was also to do with the fact that basically she was doing mothering alone. And a lot of the earlier critiques like Luise's [Eichenbaum] and mine were about reconceptualising parenting. There's a seduction that's happened. Psychoanalysis has added to our understanding of feminist therapy in very valuable ways, but it seems to me that instead of psychoanalysis being an interesting way into understanding the construction of femininity or masculinity, or instead of psychoanalysis being an account of the defence structure, instead of psychoanalysis being a way of understanding how the early relationship is internalised and what that does, psychoanalysis has discovered that you need this consistent relationship and the mother has to do the separating at a certain stage, and something else at another stage. This sounds very unthought through to me, like awfully kosher psychoanalysis with a little reformist dream added to it that women are supposed to have a bit more subjectivity than they were supposed to have before. Twenty years ago the problems in women's subjectivity were seen to have something to do with the structure of parenting and gender relations.

WH That takes us into the whole thorny issue of fathering and mothering and parenting, and what the difference is. I felt, writing my chapter, that I was caught between two contradictory political positions. One was bring fathers or surrogate fathers into the picture, and say 'mothers doing this on their own is not the same' and I particularly wanted to talk about the triangular structure there; on the other hand, this is a period where lone mothers are being castigated.

SO We've lost the critique somewhere, that parenting is impossible when it's done on a single basis. Now, you're right. Part of the reasons we've lost that critique is because of the attack on single mothers. I don't think the attack on single mothers should be about resurrecting the heterosexual nuclear family. It's not the right feminism to reinstate the father in this particular role: the father who does this and the father who does that.

PARENTING MEDIATED BY THE CHILD'S GENDERED PHANTASIES?

In my view, the most significant difference between feminist object relations theory – of which Susie is one of the best known representatives – and feminist 'cultural' psychoanalysis (which includes many disparate strands) is the role of unconscious phantasy in constructing subjectivity and therefore influencing the actual relations of any given person. This difference has been linked to another critique, namely, that feminist object relations has talked about the (actual) mother and not about the place of the father (both real and phantasy) in the child's mind (see Sayers 1995). Here we broach another crucial political, as well as theoretical, question: How much difference do the actual behaviours of parents and carers make to a child's emerging subjectivity? If fathers do just what mothers do, will it be received in the same way or mediated through unconscious phantasy? Janine Chasseguet-Smirgel (1976) argues that any child's unconscious phantasies – initially and primarily in relation to the mother's power to satisfy or deny the dependent infant's needs – affect that relationship in a way which makes it distinct from the paternal relationship. If so, we are talking about forces deeply embedded in (all) human cultures that a simple equalisation of parenting practices and responsibilities will not eradicate, though it may well help to modify gender differences in desirable directions. Susie Orbach disagrees with this position.

SO   I do think that more adults than one is extremely helpful and I do think gender is very significant. But the danger is of an implicit manifesto for good-enough mothering here. No, that's too strong; there is something about, the right thing is, what the mother has to do.

WH   In my chapter on the maternal bed, I recognised the significance of the triangle, and the structure of the triangle; the way that it's important to open out, so that we're not only talking about two-way relationships, with a mother and with a father, or another parent, or their substitutes – but that the relationship between mother and father in various ways is very important for the child, whether they live together or not.

SO   I actually don't see that children see their parents like this. A lot of parents don't handle the triangular relationship that way at all. It's just not the case. The child and the mother have one relationship and the father is excluded from it.

WH   I'd say that that was another example of a triangular issue. The political implications, though, might be that we would be aiming for even more: as well as having a good relationship with a daughter, or a son, as mothers or as fathers, the relationship with the other parent and parent figures would actually be saying something unconsciously about adult love and hate, adult sexuality, the relationships between the sexes. I know it's another burden to take on: good-enough parental relationships as well!

SO I think maybe there is a sort of idealisation of the parental relationship. I think a lot of women are burdened by their mother's dissatisfactions in the marriage – in the parental relationship.

WH Isn't that part of daughters' – particularly daughters' – perceptions of what the future is likely to hold, if her mother's dissatisfied?

SO I think contempt is a major issue. Contempt for men, contempt for your own mother for sticking with an unsatisfactory relationship.

WH Does that come up in your clinical practice?

SO Yes, a lot – the inability to detach. They feel contempt for their mother's staying and yet they discover staying; they re-run it for themselves.

WH Do fathers or non-biological mothers do very much the same job as the mother? One of the arguments would be that the mother occupies a special role – not because she needs to occupy a special role, but because of the place of the maternal figure in the unconscious of the developing child . . . .

SO But why? Why isn't that an assumption? What if you had two parents there from the beginning?

WH . . . So that the developing child will be making unconscious demands. Will they be maternal or parental then?

SO Well, my children do not make that separation.

WH They don't make different kinds of demands?

SO Well, now they do as they're older. But they didn't when they were younger. I mean even now, if they've been with one of us, they'll call the other – I'll be called dad. Or Joe will be called mum.

WH   Yes. That's quite a nice slip, isn't it?

SO   Yes. It's to do with the attachment they've had to the person for the previous few hours. I don't think in my son's psyche or my daughter's psyche, there's mum and then there's dad. I actually think there are these huge parental figures. We are different individuals and we are gendered, and therefore their identifications with each of us will be idiosyncratic. In addition, there's a whole bunch of significant others too. And there's each other. There's the sibling relationship. I don't like how psychoanalysis has been taken up by feminism: the assumption that the mother is this major figure. Well, she is if she's the only person, but she's not necessarily, if other adults parent.

GENDER IDENTITY AND ITS DEVELOPMENT

The political implications of feminist psychoanalytic views on gender development have been cast in some new lights by postmodern theory and queer theory. On the one hand, feminist postmodernists have engaged with and been influenced by psychoanalysis (for example, Judith Butler and Jane Flax). On the other hand, psychoanalytic theory has been criticised by postmodernism for its universalising tendencies – its 'grand narrative' of human subjectivity and gendered subjectivity. As usual, there are different versions of psychoanalysis at play. What is at stake, in my view, is whether – in line with postmodernism – we give up the notion of a basic coherence in subjectivity which includes a notion of a relatively stable identity which is gendered. Psychoanalysis has profoundly influenced poststructuralist and postmodernist critiques of a unitary, rational subject – putting at the heart of theories of subjectivity the unconscious, with its splits, paradoxes and contradictions. Yet there is within psychoanalysis, particularly British psychoanalysis, the belief that split, multiple, dispersed subjectivity is more a sign of mental distress than political liberation. For Kleinian psychoanalysis, the notion of the achievement of the depressive position – uncertain and fluid though that may be – supports a belief in the desirability of a coherent subjectivity; one in which good and bad (and other splits, for example gendered ones) can be acknowledged and brought together in one person (see Rustin 1991).

This debate raises issues of profound political importance in theorising gendered subjectivity. Susie Orbach makes clear her belief in the desirability of a stable gender identity from the point of view of someone's own well-being. A stable gender identity is not, however, the same thing as traditional masculinity or femininity, nor sexual practice, nor orientation. The subsequent discussion raises in particular the role of explanations in terms of unconscious socialisation by the mother or emphasis on parental sexuality and triangular relationships traditionally central to Oedipal theory of gender development.

SO: Everybody needs to have a stable gender identity. I don't think gender-bending is of any value whatsoever. It's extremely hurtful to people.

WH I agree that it can, but I think that a lot of people are very persuaded by the kind of positions that Judith Butler takes up.

SO From a clinician's perspective, they're a nonsense. I think what gets conflated often is sexually stereotyped behaviours that get built on gender. I am much more interested in what the emotional possibilities are for both genders. And at the moment we know they're constrained. And they are very sex-role stereotyped, whether you're boys or girls. So, for me, the implications for parenting and the implications for child rearing are around the emotional areas, because I still think that our daughters are being raised, unconsciously and consciously, to be far more relation-inclined, to be much more aware of the sort of emotional field around them and still to translate their own emotional distresses by taking care of others. I still see that going on all the time. I still see boys not being able to hold on to their emotional responses and having very few routes to express them except through macho and violence and aggression, or competition. I think those are really significant things.

WH Can I stop you there and ask what you think are the processes which are still leading to those differential outcomes.

SO I think part of it's an unconscious identification. Well, I can talk about myself, because I think I've done that. When my daughter started to talk – started to make sounds – I taught her conversation. I wouldn't say that I did that consciously, but I saw the sounds that she emitted as being proto-conversations, and very early on she became very skilled with language. I don't think that's unusual for girls. Now it's not that mothers don't have proto-conversations with boys, but it may not be with words. I know when my son spoke, I thought that it was so amazing that he spoke that I would reply back with the same word, rather than extend the conversation.

WH   That sounds as if you were responding to a difference in them as well.

SO   I'm sure it has an effect, but the fact is, girls are very much more articulate in certain ways and have a kind of subtlety, don't they? I think I contributed to that and to my son's more limited articulacy. So I think that's one way. What are the other kinds of processes? I observe mothers silencing daughters a lot, emotionally, I really do.

WH   Because they're too like themselves?

SO   Well that's a shorthand, but, yes, that is what I would conclude.

WH   Do you think there is any part played by maternal sexuality, by parental sexuality, in this – which is at the core of a psychoanalytic Oedipal explanation?

SO   I don't see it. I mean, I could be really blind. By sexuality do you mean the erotic?

WH   Desire for the mother – whatever you want to incorporate in that – and how boys have to have a different resolution to that desire from girls: I'm paraphrasing the Oedipus complex.

SO   I don't see it that way. I do see boys' fear of engulfment by the mother. But I don't see it necessarily in Oedipal terms.

WH   For example, take Jessica Benjamin's arguments. We have to make distinctions, in the sense that some boys grow up differently from other boys. So we've got to make distinctions about this passage through Oedipus. If boys go through a process of repudiating the mother, which means that no positive identifications with the mother are left available to the boy (and if he's had an absent father, there aren't any others) then he's bereft, certainly of nurturing identifications. To talk instead about renunciation implies working through loss, like in Klein's depressive position, in which case, you come to terms with the grief and the envy about the mother for what you can't be and have, to the point where you've come to terms with the deprivations of reality, without losing positive identifications with the mother. Something similar can be applied to girls in reverse, though it's more complicated. You can reach a point where you've accepted that you're a girl, you're not a boy. You can be certain things and not other things. That seems to me to be an important part of feminist thought about gender development.

SO   Well, I do think boys and girls occupy very different places and they have to know which gender they belong to, and I do think that they have different developmental tasks *vis-à-vis* their mothers. They are absolutely different. There's always been a problem with Chodorow's work, for me. I don't think mothers see their sons and their daughters as the same and that then all of a sudden their boys are different, and I think I read that into Benjamin's work. I've never gone along with that. So to me, it's not that boys suddenly have to do something at 18 months: they've always been different.

WH   Because the mother has unconsciously never seen them as the same?

SO   And I think it saves boys' lives actually. I think psychically it can be quite protective to boys.

WH   Are you saying, to put it technically, that the projective identifications that the mother is engaging in with her daughter don't work in the same way with the son?

SO   No, they don't.

WH   Because he's different from the start?

SO   Yes.

WH Presumably some mothers don't feel that difference as much as others?

SO I presume they don't. Or some mothers may, you know, be so thrilled that they've had a son, because they're different – or because we're still coming out of a cultural history in which sons were more valued than daughters. There are a million different reasons, but the point is, it isn't the same for the mother. It really isn't the same. A lot of parents will, say, 'Well, I treated them exactly the same.' 'But did you feel the same way about them?' 'Oh no. I gave them the same toys, but the boys went for pistols and girls went for...' 'But did you feel the same way about them? Did you have the same kind of conversations? Did you hold them the same? Are you the kind of mother who actually fed your daughters and sons the same length of time, felt equally relaxed about their appetites, potty trained them at the same time?... No, you didn't, did you? You did exactly what the whole culture does, which is you weaned the daughter early, you know, you potty trained her earlier: all of the things that we unconsciously reproduce.' But they'll say they did the same thing.

WH Supposing we have an active father in the picture, right from the start. What's going on there that may differentiate for the girl and the boy?

SO They are different people and I think that's really valuable. I don't think it's that one is the authoritarian figure and one is the nurturing figure. I've always thought the mother was the authoritarian figure anyway, within most families. The one who says 'no' much more than the father. But I think what happens is that first the strain is taken off so that the parent isn't quite so unable to tolerate the child's difficulties and isn't so frustrated. Right. And one parent may deal with the child's distress in one way and one in another. So they have a different experience of being able to metabolise the distress of the child, and I think the child will see different things in each parent. And they will see the parents as separate, and having a relationship with each other and as not only being for them, which I think is quite valuable.

WH Can we go back to the question about gender-bending?

SO Yes.

WH   As far as you're concerned, you disagree with the position that it is desirable to be free to move between gender positions – the gender performance. Is that right?

SO   I think it's a wonderful idea as performance and you know, I think it mirrors people's wish to play with gender at the level of performance, but not at the level of life. I think it's the whole problem with postmodernism. Postmodernism valorises the fragmentation that we see around us and says, 'Oh, let's play with this, let's play with that.' But I don't think it provides sufficient understanding of the crises of masculinity and femininity, which is what this gender-as-performance is about. Of course we're very constrained by what's built on top of gender and we're working very hard to try and expand our categories of what each gender can do. But I think if you don't know yourself from the inside as male or female, or masculine or feminine, it is so troublesome, that it's not a life.

WH   I agree, but I think there are different uses of psychoanalysis in postmodernist analyses of gender identity.

SO   I just read a paper of Judith Butler's recently. The psychoanalysis she's using is the psychoanalysis that nobody today uses. We read it in our study group. Now, in my study group, one of the psychotherapists works a lot with people with gender difficulties. You know guys who pin their penises to themselves – stuff that's horrible, so disabling. It isn't performance, it really isn't.

WH   Which bit of early Freud are you referring to?

SO   I don't think we were bisexual in the beginning, and then we became boys at 4. I think we were given a gender. Your daughter was given a gender. All of your unconscious went into it. You didn't see her as being both. You saw her as being one. I would accept that little kids, from my experience, don't see themselves as gendered until about 18 months. I do accept that.

WH   Eventually they have to accept, if they're going to come to terms with 'reality', that they're not a boy or they're not a girl.

SO   Absolutely. I mean I was part of that debate – whether women can be boxers; I mean, not that I give a shit about boxing, but some women can be boxers: it isn't a masculine attribute. If you go back to that notion of retrieval of the things that you lost in a bisexual paradise that I'm not sure existed, it would be to own those as a *female*, not to own those as a third gender or a cross-gender, which is very, very destabilising.

WH   Yes. To return to the issue of how rigid a gender identity boys and girls acquire. Surely one of the big issues is what they give up in terms of their introjects; in terms of the potential of their personality.

SO   If I just think of my own kids, the things that my son thought girls couldn't do, or boys couldn't do, were nothing to do with these profound things I thought they were going to be. You know, it was like daddy played tennis, then girls don't play tennis, boys play tennis. It was simply about a categorical organisation.

WH   What becomes difficult to define is what ends up being the distinction between being a man and being a woman, if everything that we can do is included in being womanly – which it should be, in principle.

SO   Biology. I mean our capacity to reproduce and theirs to impregnate, isn't that it? I do think that is it. I don't think it's more than that. I do think those are fundamental differences, though, because I think they affect every way you relate to your body.

WH   Might that not also mean that children will have a different relationship to their mother because they were born of her, and probably breast-fed by her, for example in terms of phantasies of power and dependency, and therefore there will be connections that will never be the case for the father?

SO   We don't know yet because we don't have a mass alternative to the family. We really don't know. Yes, your point is well-taken. But we must find out about fathers who did a lot of holding: they didn't do feeding, but they did a lot of holding, what place do they occupy in terms of phantasies of power and dependency?

FEMINIST PSYCHOTHERAPY

A similar gender-conscious understanding of the psychodynamic forces involved in mother–child relations informs feminist psychotherapists' methods and their understanding of what is going on in the relationship between the therapist and client, or patient, at an unconscious level (the transference and counter-transference relationship). Susie Orbach and Luise Eichenbaum have been involved in a long-running debate regarding mother–daughter transferences within the therapist–client relationship. They summarise the common difficulties of women from a wide variety of backgrounds in therapy as follows: 'the most striking feature of our work with women... was the deep shame, resistance and confusion which coalesced around the issues of dependency, neediness and desire for attachment' (Orbach and Eichenbaum, 1995: 89). Recent theory in feminist clinical psychoanalysis which develops ideas about the therapist's role has meant emphasising the therapist's subjectivity rather than her ability to be a blank screen for the client's transferences: 'We understood that the therapist was not only object but subject as well. And moreover, for both women and men patients, the experience of the subjectivity of the female therapist was essential to the project of change' (ibid.: 95). These theoretical discussions concerning psychotherapeutic practice are part of the same developments which have enabled debates on mothering to conceptualise an autonomous maternal subject whose autonomy signifies not just the recognition of a woman's independent desires, but her capacity to recognise those of her children, that is, to distinguish them from her own and to act accordingly: 'the position of the therapist being a selfless, idealized other was now under scrutiny' (ibid).

WH   I'd like to ask you about the direction of feminist therapy: where you'd like to see it going, what its doing and what its role is in the wider feminist movement.

SO   I still think feminism has a lot to say. A gender-conscious therapy really does transform how you understand psychoanalysis. And I think that's still not widely disseminated. I think that you'll see clinicians pushing for women to separate because they know that women don't separate, and that's the clinical issue. But they haven't understood that women didn't separate because the basis of the attachment was so problematic in the first place and that if you push a woman to separate, what you are doing is reinforcing her defence structure, rather than deconstructing a false separation.

WH   Is that your definition of what a gender-conscious analysis would bring to psychotherapy?

SO   It would be one of the features. Another feature would be that it would understand how complicated women find issues of dependency and issues of emotional recognition: that we may crave those, but that we've got very high-level defence structures that defend against those cravings being perceived. I think if you're not gender-conscious, you don't get that people are resisting and it looks much easier than it is. And people tell you they're much better and 'thank you very much', and they don't want to be a trouble.

WH   You say a gender-conscious analysis, does that have implications for the treatment of men as well?

SO   Oh, absolutely.

WH   Of what kind?

SO   Well, I think it's quite possible that, in the therapy, you could unwittingly reinforce men's defensive separation too, by being interested in their acts of autonomy, as opposed to going through the pain and struggle of them facing their fears of closeness and intimacy. I'm not saying that everybody would, but I think it's quite easy to do that.

WH   By not being conscious of the different approaches to the issues of separation and connectedness that men and women come with?

SO   Exactly. Also, there are issues around sexuality, which may have a lot to do with how men organise their emotional life. Feminism has influenced me sufficiently that I am amazed that issues that men may still have around sexuality aren't expanded into who they are in other areas. Therapists have to do a lot of different things, but one is being able to withstand in therapy all of the attacks and disappointments that a daughter had experienced. So that you were, not a perfect mother, but you were the mother who could withstand the attack and you could tolerate it and you could withstand the destruction, you would be somebody who could manage and absorb. You could let the person get through their distress. But in that model you wouldn't present a different persona particularly. You were the patient's object rather than a subject in your own right. I think the shift now is to insist on your own subjectivity.

WH   How do you do that as a therapist?

SO   Well, I think it's linked up with another bit of psychoanalysis. In the last twenty years the most important developments in psychoanalysis have been around understanding the person who's in therapy from the perspective of reading the counter-transference: what the therapist feels at any given moment in the therapy. Particularly what you might call a kind of wild-cat counter-transference: why you're feeling something that's so out of phase with the content that's being discussed. So the work on counter-transference had been to see it as a reflection of what is created by the patient in the therapy relationship. In the last few years it's been seen not as a creation of the patient, but the co-creation of the therapist and the patient. You wouldn't get the same counter-transference with anybody else. It is absolutely something that you create together. Now, if that's the cutting edge of understanding psychoanalytic practice, it brings in the subjectivity of the therapist, so that the therapist is always reflecting upon how she or he is influencing and being influenced by what's happening. I think you introduce it in a very simple way by saying, 'Oh, this may sound quite odd to you, but while you're saying this, I've been thinking X, would this be of any use to us in our discussion?' Or it might be, 'Is there another way we can look at it from my point of view?' Either way, it would mean owning it.

WH   Yes, you're not just wherever they want you to be.

SO   Yes. Now obviously you've to think very carefully about why you're thinking that. Because you're not there just to think your own thoughts! So you've got to be careful and say, 'Look, while you're saying this, I'm thinking that you're asking, can I look after you in a certain kind of way. You're yearning for X, Y, and Z.' And that's one level that's going out. On another level I'm feeling this and I'm wondering what that has to do with the dynamic. I think we'd be adding to the conversation. It ties up with Benjamin's points about recognition or our point [i.e. LE and SO] about what we used to call dependency, which I suppose we would call recognition now: being able to tolerate what the other person is asking of you, without requiring that you disappear within that.

WH Can you just make clear how the shift occurred in your thinking, from dependency to recognition.

SO Well, I think we used to argue – and I still believe this – that, to a very large extent, girls are brought up to have a complicated relationship to the omission of their own desires; omission of their own needs, because of the inconsistent relating, and because of the identification between mothers and daughters, that mothers are unable to tolerate certain kinds of distress in their daughters, or certain kinds of initiatives and desires. We used to call that dependency needs.

WH And once it's called recognition?

SO It isn't different, but I think it's a different way of talking about it. We never thought you had to meet the dependency in therapy, even though we were often criticised for being gratifiers. We were never able to do so anyway. But we did feel that the history of not being comfortable with women's dependency needs is also the history of women not feeling comfortable with needs emanating from themselves, and therefore feeling very insecure all the time, creating either a person that was very clingy, or one who appeared to have no needs whatsoever. It's also women's language: 'I'm so dependent.' 'I just want to be independent.' 'I'm fine when I'm not with somebody because I don't have any needs.' 'The minute I'm with somebody I'm so needy.' So I think the language came very much out of the language of our patients, or our clients.

WOMEN'S GROUPS

Group therapy with women has always played an important part in the specifically feminist provision of therapeutic help (see Chapter 10). This is partly because of the important history of consciousness-raising groups within the Women's Liberation Movement and partly because of the strong tradition of group analytic work within clinical

psychoanalysis. Group psychotherapy works with the difficult uncon-
scious dynamics that women are likely to bring, while consciousness-
raising groups, inspired by the political principle of women's liberation
from traditional constraints, may stand for the triumph of sisterhood,
no matter what goes on under the surface. In this extract, Susie
Orbach and I explore these visions of women working together in
groups in terms of mother–daughter dynamics.

SO   You have all these tensions in a mother–daughter relationship.
But this wonderful thing about women's groups – women's therapy
groups – is extending and expanding what can happen between
women, the kind of healing that goes on. Not simply from the
mother–daughter metaphor, but from woman to woman. That
you actually can transcend mother–daughter dynamics.

WH   The defining feature of the woman-to-woman relationship,
or you might say sisterhood, would it then be the healing that could
go on?

SO   Yes. Because I think there is so much longing and so much
desire and so much wish to trust and not be betrayed and not be
abandoned – all of those issues between mothers and daughters
which get played out in woman-to-woman relationships. But I
don't think that the only metaphor is in terms of mother–daughter
relationships. I think that in the group, they are all adult women
with all their vulnerabilities and all their strengths and they are
capable of knowing what each other requires, and of working
together to be connected but in a way detached at the same time.

WH   I can see that when the group is having difficulties, you can
analyse the dynamics in terms of the things that go wrong in
mother–daughter relationships. Sometimes the group transcends
those difficulties, which at times is very satisfying and pleasurable.
But I don't understand why you shift the terminology and say it's no
longer about the mother–daughter relationship, as if that will only
hold for the difficulties.

SO   Of course, the positive side is also about mothers and daughters. But I don't think parents and children should have relationships of equality – if that's the right way to put it: I don't think
parents and children should be best friends. I don't think that is

what inter-generational relationships are about. I do think parents are about providing certain things so that children can grow themselves up well enough to become adults and that parents need to continue to grow. You may become very close when you're older, and you may be very close and intimate when you're being a parent, but it's not about being best friends.

WH   Yes, you're not in an equivalent position to do so.

SO   Absolutely not. Now in a group there's a difference. There is all the transference material and the unconscious material – and the part of you that's the mother and the daughter. But there is also you as a bunch of equal, adult women, managing differences among equals, which I think is so beautiful about the learning experience in a women's group.

REFERENCES

Chasseguet-Smirgel, J. (1976) 'Freud and Female Sexuality', *International Journal of Psychoanalysis*, 57: 275–86.

Orbach, S. and Eichenbaum, L. (1995) 'From Objects to Subjects', *British Journal of Psychotherapy*, 12(1): 89–97.

Rustin, M. (1991) *The Good Society and the Inner World: Psychoanalysis, Politics and Culture*, London: Verso.

Sayers, J. (1995) 'Consuming Male Fantasy: Feminist Psychoanalysis Retold', in A. Elliott and S. Frosh (eds) *Psychoanalysis in Contexts: Paths between Theory and Modern Culture*, London: Routledge: 123–41.

Chapter 7

The heaven and hell of mothering
Mothering and ambivalence in the mass media

Ros Coward

The family snapshot of a murdered child has become one of the most forceful icons of a decade preoccupied by its own failure to maintain a baseline of moral decency. Pictures of children in their homes and schools represent an innocence and security which we have failed to protect, like the class pictures of the murdered children of Dunblane embodying an unimaginable violation of places of security and protection. Certain images even become a shorthand for the moral anxiety stirred up by tragic events, like the face of 2-year-old James Bulger. His smiling tilted face on the corner of numerous articles on violence and children became a symbol of a profound moral crisis. Perhaps more than any other images, these photos sum up a fundamental problem in modern society: they ask how have we allowed hate to violate love?

Whenever children are murdered, newspapers print such family snapshots and these are always unbearably poignant. But there is something especially difficult when the children are victims of their own mothers. In the early 1990s, a series of such murders meant that photos like these regularly made the front pages of most of the British newspapers. They are always of the children at their cutest, or at landmark moments in the child's development. And, as evidence of the photographer's pride and love, not hate, they are deeply troubling. Whereas images of James Bulger or the children of Dunblane are images of parents' protective love violated, the images of children killed by their own mothers confront us with the possibility that a mother might both love and hate her children. They hint at a maternal ambivalence which our culture normally denies.

On both sides of the Atlantic, these troubling images are now occurring more frequently. The case of Susan Smith affected

Americans in the same way as the James Bulger case affected the British. It symbolised an encounter with previously unimaginable depravity. Not only had a mother killed her child, but she appeared to have calculated the deed and then lied to cover it up. Susan Smith, a member of a small, ostensibly peaceful, community in Carolina claimed her children had been 'car-napped' by 'blacks'. She made several emotional appeals on national television supported by the local pastor, who prayed publicly with her during the first days of the little boys' disappearance. Eventually Susan Smith confessed that she had strapped her two children, 3-year-old Michael and 14-month-old Alex, into their car seats before rolling the car into a lake.

In the months immediately after Susan Smith's arrest, much press attention was given to similar murders. And there was no shortage. Almost immediately afterwards, two young Tennessee children were found suffocated in intense heat, also strapped into car seats. They had been left by a mother while she went to a party at a local hotel. Another mother, Pauline Zile, was charged as accomplice to the murder of her 9-year-old daughter. She had been beaten to death, in Zile's presence, by the girl's stepfather. In the same week, a Long Island woman was charged with killing her 2-year-old son by punching him so hard that he bled to death from internal injuries.

These were not isolated incidents. In the United States, the number of child murders has increased rapidly over the last forty years. The number of children under 1 year who are killed has doubled, and has quadrupled for those between the ages of 1 and 4. More than twenty in every 100,000 black children are killed. Sixty per cent of those charged are the parents, casting a whole new light on the term 'blood relations' and requiring that we reconsider the usual perception that children are more at risk from strangers than from their own relatives.

The same trend is apparent in Britain, although the figures are proportionately smaller. It is not surprising that, in the light of a summer like 1995 when five children were murdered, including one girl abducted from a tent in a garden and two boys stabbed on a fishing expedition, many parents restrict their children's mobility, fearful of stranger danger. But this concentration created a false impression. On average only six children are killed each year by strangers. The majority of children killed in Britain are still killed by relatives and, if recent reports are to be believed, the numbers may be higher than those given officially[1].

Yet, maltreatment of a child by its own mother is always news-worthy and is presented as the ultimate incomprehensible act. The attitude of the tabloid media is summed up in the coverage of a story of an abandoned child in February 1996. The *Daily Mail* filled its entire front page with a picture of the newborn baby found abandoned hours after his birth at Heathrow airport. The massive headline asked simply, 'How Could A Mother Dump Him?' Much of the horror of the trial of Rosemary West was focused on the murder of her 8-year-old stepdaughter and her own 14-year-old daughter Heather. Ordinary family snapshots again created troub-ling discontinuities with information about the torture and abuse these children probably experienced before their deaths.

In the last few years more mundane cases have been given a great deal of prominence in the press. In May 1995, Joyce Senior stabbed her three children to death in Norfolk, before killing herself. Several tabloids gave their front pages over to the story, illustrated by a large family snapshot of the children. Eight-year-old Benjamin Slowley and his 2-year-old brother Samuel were also given the front page of the *Daily Mail*, smiling and posing proudly in match-ing outfits. They were found strangled and their mother was arrested. In the same year Celia Beckett was convicted of killing one of her daughters and poisoning another; again the case was illustrated by a lovely family portrait of the murdered child.

One word crops up time and again in the press coverage of child murders: 'evil'. In the James Bulger case, the photos used were located underneath headlines like: 'Evil', 'Wicked', 'Unparalleled Evil'. Ironically, these photos of the two boys who had committed the murder were the same type as those of the murdered children. They were images of children scrubbed for school, presented by (at least occasionally) proud parents to the school photographer to capture them at their best. This coexistence of 'evil' in 'innocence' signified a profound moral crisis, a destruction of the innocence of childhood. The degeneracy of the boys, their terrible act and their victim, together were seen as the boys having killed the innocence of themselves.

But what could be worse than a mother who violates the inno-cence she is meant to protect? In America, this discourse of incom-prehensible evil came to the fore in the case of Susan Smith. Although the press provided lurid details of her unhappy life (she was violently abused herself as a child, and lived a life of poverty and desperation), few considered these to be extenuating

circumstances. The press framed her unhappy life in terms of evil
choices, extensively quoting the pastor who had been tricked into
helping her. He said that however wretched her life, she had committed an 'evil deed', choosing to listen to Satan rather than God on
the night she drowned her children.

In the 1960s and 1970s the Enlightenment belief that understanding such lives might lead us to forgive would have had at least an
equal hearing. But now there appears to have been a significant
shift. Maury, the chat-show host quoted in the *New York Times
Magazine* at the time of the Susan Smith murders, says that the
balance tipped at the time of the Menendez brothers' trial:

> That was the crushing blow for the whole abuse defense. That
> jolted audiences. There's been a backlash. Abuse defenses are
> now looked at cynically and audiences are falling back on old
> beliefs in good and evil.

This shift can be explained partly by a simultaneous increase in acts
of extreme violence and a growing exploitation of abuse as a
defense. But in part this return to fundamentalist notions of good
and evil has been whipped up by the Right. The Right in America
has been active in campaigning against more forgiving interpretations of human behaviour, framing poor lives such as Susan Smith's
in terms of 'evil'. They see evil as a fundamental condition of
humanity which gets the upper hand in a society which has abandoned traditional morality in favour of seeking self-satisfaction.
Newt Gingrich asserted that Susan Smith's boys died because of
the libertarian, 'me first' society, spawned by the 1960s. As a single
mother whose new boyfriend had just ditched her because he wasn't
ready to take on responsibilities, her deeds were interpreted as
trying to square the circle of her own selfish interests.

The Tennessee mother, Jennie Bain, whose children suffocated in a
locked car, was 20 and another single mother. In Britain, an article in
the *Daily Telegraph* entitled 'Parent First, Child Last' used Gingrich's 'me first' interpretation of her lethal mistake, describing how
Jennie Bain left her children outside to die in suffocating heat, while
she partied. The journalist Charles Laurence went on to link the
deaths of these two boys with other recent murders of children by
their mothers:

> At the heart of the issue is a crisis of motherhood. There is a
> dissonance in contemporary culture: generations have been

reared on the principal of instant gratification and the "me first" interpretation of the much vaunted constitutional right to the "pursuit of happiness". How do children fit into that?'

(*Daily Telegraph*, June 1995)

In both the USA and the UK, evil is the only concept possible when children have come to embody society's sense of itself as good. Children are the place where the best of humanity is expressed. They appear free from the corruptions of the world and they elicit from those around them the nobler emotions of protectiveness and love. Any attack on this innocence is seen as coming from outside the relationship between adult and child – an outside force, which is named 'evil'. But in all these murders there was much more at stake than evil selfishness. This comes across, not just from the photos but from the troubling details of these murders. Both Susan Smith's and Jennie Bain's little children were strapped into *safety* seats. Like the photos, concern with the children's safety is evidence that the mother's protective love was once in place. These images and information seem to tell us, not of simple wickedness but confusion, ambivalence, the dual presence of love and hate, mental disturbance. What comes over is not evil, but women whose intellectually and emotionally impoverished visions, and whose lack of real social support, gave them no way out of their crazy decisions.

These impoverished lives, limited horizons and unsupported delusions are what come across in the accounts of the lives of mothers involved in recent child murders in England. In the majority of the more high-profile cases, the women have been single mothers. Joyce Senior and Tracey Rutherford (the mother of Benjamin and Sam Slowley) had recently separated from their partners, and neighbours and friends knew that the separations had been traumatic. Many are like Celia Beckett, with a long history of contact with the social services. She was a single mother graded at two points above mental handicap, and social services had believed her hysterical account of her children's accidents and illnesses, seeing her initially as a victim requiring support. Only later, with a greater knowledge of Munchausen's syndrome, was it recognised that she was damaging her children herself. In a recent case, a young couple set fire to their home hoping to claim off the insurance but unwittingly killed one child and severely injured another. They were described as mentally limited and poor, living chaotic and disordered lives.

Rather than visions of evil, what emerges are pictures of delusions amounting to mental illness, where hostility towards children is often out of control. But they also conjure up pictures of intolerable stresses, particularly stresses caused by loneliness and lack of help with the children. In both of the notorious American cases, it was possible to see young inadequate women with sole responsibility for tiny children and no-one to turn to. Neither seemed to have relatives or friends who might have offered them ways out of their predicaments. In killing their children, or letting them die, their actions were undoubtedly extreme, but many mothers might recognise elements of the picture – intolerable pressures, the burdens of responsibility in situations where there is no help and, indeed, occasional feelings of hostility.

There used to be a public discourse about the fact that, without real support, motherhood is the most high-pressure job there is. Feminism, in its early days, talked of how unsupported motherhood could, quite literally, drive you crazy. Fay Weldon's novels were full of mothers who, if not exactly child murderers, were at least seriously awry. *Down Among the Women* was a founding text of feminism and showed women isolated, frustrated and exhausted with the task of looking after small children. This demystification of the joys of self-sacrificing motherhood was crucial in the formulation of feminist politics. It led feminists to call for men to be more involved in parenting, for the state to provide better child-care facilities, and for the provision of proper benefits for mothers who lost the support of men.

Yet throughout the 1980s this discourse was eroded. It was partly feminism's own fault. Having at first concentrated on the negative or difficult aspects of mothering, feminism seemed to have nothing to say about the deep satisfactions that mothering can bring. Antifeminists also categorised feminists as whingeing, selfish careerists bent on destroying the family. A reaction set in. During the 1980s, motherhood was romanticised again, so much so that the '*Kinder und Kuche*' images of the 1950s now look like social realism.

Some of this romanticism came from within feminism itself. Women who had delayed becoming mothers while concentrating on political action and careers, now discovered motherhood with a vengeance. They began to recast the problematic. It was not so much that motherhood was bad, but that it was insufficiently valued. In the 1980s, unlike the 1970s, this recognition would involve an elevation of maternal status commensurate with the new status of women; motherhood would be seen as a difficult job that was an important, satisfying and pleasurable aspect of women's lives. Together with a continued concern with the importance of women's careers, this produced a new emphasis on the working mother – her satisfactions, problems and dilemmas. In the context of the increasing demand for women workers, of which mothers made up the most obvious area of expansion, being a working mother became not only fashionable but heroic.

Outside feminism, this new emphasis on motherhood ignored the difficulties and problems. Instead, public figures – actresses, news-readers, politicians – were shown with their children. If the heroic and fashionable ideal for women was being a working mother, it became almost *de rigueur* for celebrities to parade the fact that they too fulfilled the necessary criteria. Away from feminism, the empha-sis was on women maintaining their looks and figures, in order to signal the fact that having children did not spell the end of an exciting social or sexual life.

In the popular media, motherhood was '*Hello!*ed', reduced to photo opportunities of glamorous and successful mothers, chatter-ing about their perfect children who were perfect fun to be with, and who deepened their perception of life. In this version, motherhood is having small human accessories while staying unchanged. Demi Moore, posing naked eight months pregnant, suggests that even three children will not change her body or her active available sexuality. Paula Yates has been continually in the public eye, some-times modelling underwear, sometimes demonstrating her active sexuality, but often talking about her children and her desire to have more. Her children's names – Fifi Trixibelle, Peaches and Little Pixi and Heavenly – seem somehow like an acknowledgement, albeit in questionable taste, that they are indeed the ultimate accessories.

Motherhood is made to look so easy, as if there's nothing involved – no work, no money and certainly no ambivalent feelings. Contemporary feminism, fighting a rearguard action, has only been able to say that single or working mothers can have it all too. Anyone who dares say that mothering is difficult and stressful feels dowdy and inadequate. If Ruby Wax, Jennifer Saunders and Nicola Horlicks can have a clutch of children, and glorious careers, how dare the rest of us moan and complain? How can anyone talk of difficulties and conflict when public figures under immense career pressures can carry it off with such apparent ease?

Feminism in the 1970s may have been wrong to present mother-hood as all hell; but it's not all heaven either. Mothering is difficult. It demands changes in your life and it changes you, sometimes unleashing feelings that can quite literally drive you crazy. Women can find themselves up against unexpected emotions of anger and gnawing guilt, instead of living up to the idealised version of good-ness poured out to good children. Mothers need support, particu-larly if they are on their own. Yet this current idealisation of motherhood denies women the chance to come to terms with the confusing mixture of emotions that motherhood involves. Sadly, the only public acknowledgement comes in the most tragic form, in the photographs of dead children, once loved enough to be recorded but now hated enough to be obliterated.

This maternal ambivalence presents profound problems for our culture. Childhood is the benchmark of our innocence, and parents' fierce protectiveness is a symbol of our culture's desire to protect that. It is the sign of our decency. The despair caused by the killing of children is the despair that we have not been able to keep safe the most cherished part of ourselves. When it is done to the child by those with the most reason to keep that child safe, the despair is greater. In that context, it is not surprising that commentators reach out for 'evil' as an explanation. Unfortunately, in doing so, many women are deprived of ways of understanding their own feelings. They are cheated of ways of recognising when they should go for help.

NOTE

1. In March 1996, a report was presented to a conference in London by John Fitzgerald, director of the Bridge, an independent child-care con-sultancy. In it, Fitzgerald claimed that many deaths from neglect were going unreported, partly because it had become unfashionable to suspect it: 'I do not think there is a will to collect these statistics in a meaningful way. There is currently a belief that children do not die of neglect: therefore it is not looked for' (quoted in the *Guardian*, March 1996).

Chapter 8

In the company of women
Experiences of working with the lost mother

Paddy Maynes and Joanna Best

Whilst meeting to plan and discuss the writing of this chapter, we found ourselves reflecting upon why it has taken eleven years to begin to record publicly the clinical work undertaken at Islington Women's Counselling Centre (IWCC). The clients, coming as they do from poor white and ethnic minority communities, are multiply deprived and, being so, they are often deemed marginal, representing the objects rather than the subjects of society. Like our clients, we, as analytic counsellors, have rendered ourselves marginal to and invisible within the psychotherapeutic world. Just as our clients have felt compelled to hide their struggles to withstand and survive violent and abusive past and present relationships, so too have we hidden our therapeutic relationships. Perhaps we feared that, by constantly holding in focus our clients' external worlds and external objects whilst simultaneously focusing on the way these external realities impacted on their psychic constellations, we might not be 'good-enough' counsellors. The shame and invisibility experienced by our clients became felt and experienced by those who work with them.

IWCC was established in the midst of a void, when in 1984 a group of feminists met to discuss, lament and reflect upon the predominance of working-class and ethnic minority women patients within the psychiatric system. Through their work in front-line agencies as community, health or social workers, they had witnessed the absence of economically accessible alternatives to psychiatric care – in particular, the absence of free counselling for economically deprived women. Their concern, with regard to this lack, was transformed into action. A decade and a half later IWCC has evolved from an anti-psychiatry, consciousness-raising group into a professionally staffed, multi-ethnic and, most importantly, free analytic counselling centre. The core of the Centre's work is the provision of free, one-to-one, psychoanalytic counselling, offered once a week, for a maximum period of one year.

As a result of the very specific targeting of IWCC's services – to women on incomes below £4,000 per annum and without degree-level education – we are reaching women who would not normally gain access to analytic counselling. These criteria have formed the bedrock of IWCC's philosophy since its inception. Our client group is predominantly comprised of women who have experienced either severe deprivation or abuse – racial, physical and sexual. A high proportion of those women with children are bringing them up alone and 60 per cent of our clients are from ethnic minority or migrant communities. We work therapeutically with women who have the least resources and who, paradoxically, are also those to whom the least is offered. They are also a group of women consistently demonised in the media, who are expected to give unstintingly of themselves in caring for their families. Like our clients, we struggle to repair and make good an imperfect, often downright neglectful and abusive parent embodied by society or the state. We recognise the damage done, but we also do something which can be much harder for our clients to achieve: by our very existence, being visibly both female and counsellors, we represent a belief and recognition in the existence of hope and the capacity to change. We represent another image of self. The selfhood which the women achieve may *include* motherhood, but it can be different from that of their own mothers.

The counsellors working at the Centre are not simply clinicians, but are 'ambassadors' for a belief in the efficacy of psychoanalytic counselling. Most have a personal interest in, or experience of, the group of women they work with, each being committed to a particular area of expertise – for example, working with Black women, Irish women, or those in violent relationships. Counsellors cultivate close liaison with those community organisations working with their client group, thereby exemplifying that 'the analyst's concern is not just with the individual but with the interaction between the individual and his environment, starting with the family group in infancy and extending to larger groups' (Segal 1995: 191).

IWCC provides the client not merely with a dyadic relationship but with one which is multi-layered and multi-supportive in striving to acknowledge that 'this type of mother-work recognises that individual survival, empowerment and identity require group survival, empowerment and identity' (Hill Collins 1994: 59). Whilst holding in mind the primacy of our concern for the client, we believe that IWCC's proactive relationship with the community mirrors our recognition of the woman's place within her family and within her wider social context. This is especially pertinent to women from ethnic minority communities where individual and group health can be indivisible. By keeping in mind the need for an external holding environment, we are able to offer counselling to women who may require several layers of support in order for them to feel contained, and therefore able to use therapeutic intervention. Social services, primary health care professionals and community organisations form a large proportion of our referrers. Whilst maintaining client confidentiality, IWCC ensures that, if necessary, these supports and others are in place during the counselling contract, with continuous acknowledgement between counsellor and client that these supports exist and have value.

Likewise, the availability of creche facilities at IWCC demonstrates a recognition that unless a safe environment for their children is provided, some women would be unable to use counselling for themselves. When thinking about this provision we sought to acknowledge the reality for our client group – that is, the desperate shortage of affordable child care – whilst at the same time continuing to think psychodynamically about how such provision may be experienced by the clients, for example, by being aware that if a woman uses the creche for her children, it may have an impact on whether she can express her ambivalence towards them with her counsellor. The presence of our clients' children in the creche has heightened our awareness of our struggle as counsellors to keep in mind the primacy of our focus on the women as our clients, rather than their children. As we hear how our clients' distress went unheeded in childhood, we can be simultaneously confronted by both their own and their child's current pain too.

Just as recognition of the importance of the external context and supports is essential to the counsellor–client dyad, we also came to recognise the importance of group support to the counsellors. Supervision provides another layer of containment. In working with clients who have been abused and are themselves abusers, we must be aware of the prime importance of containers for ourselves as clinicians. The container facilitates the ability to think creatively about the conflicts aroused in the work and minimises the dangers of such conflicts being acted out. The change from individual to group supervision allows us to recognise the high levels of deprivation and abuse we are working with without becoming overwhelmed. It reminds us of the containment of the organisation; that we are not facing the pain of deprived and abused clients alone as an individual practitioner or supervisor. Furthermore, the supervision group brings to the clinical work a rich diversity of perspective in relation to age, race, culture and experience, mirroring the community from which our clients are drawn.

In contrast to many organisations providing psychotherapy or counselling, and in contrast to our place within that world, IWCC strives to be highly visible within this community. The effect of this is to counter the secrecy and mystique surrounding counselling/psychotherapy: a mystique which requires potential clients to make enormous efforts in order to gain access to the healthy and active part of themselves which can seek out this kind of help. The professional referrer can embody these aspects, yet there are many women who do not have contact with such professionals, or for whom such professionals would not regard counselling as appropriate. In order to achieve our avowed aim of making analytic counselling accessible to those women traditionally viewed as being 'unsuitable' for such therapeutic intervention – working-class and ethnic minority women – IWCC recognised that the counselling staff would need to mirror, to some extent, the clients' backgrounds. By demonstrating that we recognise the specific pains and pleasures of being a woman, of being Black, of being Irish, IWCC also indicates that the therapeutic space we provide is relevant and responsive to the different identities and experiences of women. In the same way that a mother signals to her baby that she recognises its existence as a separate being, a being with a multitude of unique experiences which are separate from her and recognised by her as such, we are signalling that we recognise and can bear to think about the state of being an economically deprived woman, a Black woman, an Irish woman. There is a recognition that we 'have to suffer along with the patient, but not suffer like the patient', and this recognition requires us to draw a fine line between acknowledging the specific experience and pain of our clients and yet not rendering ourselves ineffective by over-identifying and merging with them (Noonan 1983: 68).

Whilst we had hoped and expected to attract women from groups traditionally invisible in relation to such provision, what we had not expected, and initially perhaps found hard to acknowledge, was the high proportion of women we were seeing who had suffered, and in some cases were continuing to suffer, physical violence and sexual abuse. Together with early abandonment, these are by far the most commonly experienced traumas. Sometimes women speak of these experiences as simply part of life – and we have to remain alert to the signs of pain and anger which can be hidden or denied. Indeed, these painful experiences can be primarily felt as unbearable for the counsellors, who may feel drawn to collude in the denial of pain. Being aware of the power of such unbearable feelings, we are aware also of how clients sometimes need us to carry these feelings for them: this therapeutic dyad mirroring the primal dyad of mother/ infant. Frequently, the exchange within the counsellor–client dyad 'depicts a crucial process that takes place between mother and child in early infancy. The baby projects, along with love, unbearable feelings into the mother who "detoxifies" these feelings, makes sense of them for the baby in her mind, enabling the baby to feel understood, and in turn to develop her or his capacity to understand' (Bion cited in Parker 1995: 97).

The idealisation of mothering is clearly depicted in the phantasies which those outside of IWCC (as well as those of us working within it) can create around the image of a women's counselling centre. These phantasies range from an all-embracing and welcoming, accepting 'mother' – which is seemingly confirmed when, for example, we offer a woman a counselling space – to a cold, cruel and rejecting one, when we have to acknowledge the reality of our limited resources and turn a woman away. These phantasies relating to the Centre are a mirror image of the idealisation and concomitant denigration of mothering and all things female in the culture. Despite the fact that our clients have often deliberately sought out a 'women's' organisation, the idealisation that can emerge in the work is not of the significant women in their lives, but of the men, frequently abusive men. Perhaps, in seeking out a woman counsellor, they have unconsciously sought a strong and also idealised maternal figure who, they phantasise, will finally mete out punishment and prove strong enough to survive the punishment that they themselves wished to mete out to their abusers. As clinicians we have to remain alert to the danger of setting ourselves up as an idealised, perfect and omnipotent mother, always ready to take in the most needy and damaged of clients. Just as our clients can sometimes find it hard to differentiate themselves from their children, so too, we must remain aware of the dangers of over-identifying with our female clients. Both our clinical experience and our experience of working in a women's organisation, in a small yet culturally diverse team, have taught us something about the unrealistic expectations which we, as women, can place upon ourselves, our colleagues and even our clients.

We have come to understand that it is not enough to get women into the consulting room, but that we must communicate a sense of understanding to them in such a way that they are able to receive it, believing that an interpretation's 'correctness [is] . . . as much a question of its hearability as its truth in some more psychodynamic or general sort of way' (Alvarez 1992: 79). Winnicott used the analogy of the mother–baby interaction in talking about the importance of *how* the analyst offers an interpretation: 'the analyst is always groping . . . trying to find out what . . . is the shape and form of the thing he has to offer the patient' (quoted in First 1994: 150). Whilst we acknowledge the value of therapeutic boundaries, we also have to provide an experience of 'active mothering' for the women we see. Ferenczi, writing about how analysts can sometimes re-evoke the unbearable memory of an earlier abandonment for their clients, pleads for a measure of 'maternal friendliness' in therapeutic work, and in so doing, provides an alternative to the traditional 'blank screen' therapist (Ferenczi 1933: 160). In working with women who, as a result of their experiences of multiple abuse and high levels of deprivation may feel unable to hope that there could be an understanding of the impact of their external worlds on their inner worlds, we have found Anne Alvarez's writings about her work with disturbed children invaluable. She speaks about the need for the therapist to access an active aspect of maternal transference, of 'awakening' the client and how important it can be for the baby's existence to be confirmed in the mother's responses. By indicating that the 'alerting and arousing functions are as significant as soothing ones' (Alvarez 1992: 61), Alvarez aptly describes a central tenet of IWCC's clinical work, in that we often feel that we have to 'awaken' the client's long-deadened desire to be met, recognised and confirmed. It may, at times, be necessary for the counsellor to help a woman build on her strengths, whilst holding in mind the unconscious processes. Active mothering includes the ability to *think*, and Parker, in remarking on Bion's view of the importance of the mother's capacity to think about her infant, aptly describes how we may have to 'receive the full impact' of our clients' projections (Bion cited in Parker 1995: 97). As counsellors hearing and feeling the full sweep of a woman's experience of motherhood we are 'forced to reflect deeply on the meaning of motherhood for each particular woman' (Parker: personal communication, 1995).

Signs of the clients' developing capacity to understand, coupled with a concomitant high degree of psychic pain, can be manifested, for those women who are also mothers, in the relationships with their children. The point of pain which often brings a woman to seek out and use the therapeutic space is when her child is expressing a level of distress which she can identify as a mirror of her own; 'I don't want to pass it on' being a familiar acknowledgement of a growing awareness of unhappiness. A significant proportion of women receiving counselling at the Centre have children who are undergoing treatment via child guidance units or NHS psychiatric services. Statutory services, overstretched as they are, can only begin to address the child's pain, but there is little space for a woman who is in need of therapeutic help *unless it is in relation to the perceived success or failure of her mothering*. Basing our practice upon the central belief 'that seeing the mother as a subject, a person with her own needs, feelings, and interests, is critical to fighting against the dread and the devaluation of women' (Bassin, Honey and Mahrer Kaplan 1994: 2), IWCC strives to help its women clients to achieve subjectivity by providing a space into which they are received. Often the women have rarely experienced being valued and it is no surprise when they use that space to speak bitterly of how the traditional concentration on the child's needs has left them feeling excluded and pushed aside, arousing painful recollections from their own childhood. Benjamin, when speaking of the woman who 'despairs of ever holding the attention or winning the recognition of the other, of being securely held in the other's mind' (Benjamin 1988: 72), foreshadowed Tania who lamented, 'Sometimes I feel as though the wind could blow right through me, that there's nothing there.'

Many of the women we work with are bringing up children alone, or may have absent or violent partners. Whilst there are exceptions, the burden of emotional and physical care for these children falls almost exclusively upon the woman herself. Sole parenting can be one of the few arenas in which a woman experiences herself as having a measure of control, and where she feels loved. As one young woman, raised in a series of foster homes, put it, 'Getting pregnant with Jadine meant I could have something of my own'. These words are a painful reminder that many of our clients actively experience a lack of subjectivity and feel as though they never have had anything or anyone of their own. Whilst their external and internal space may be experienced as impoverished, it can also be plundered at will. Mary, a Black woman who had been multiply sexually abused from the age of 6, spoke despairingly: 'I'm just there for the taking'. What is surprising and moving to behold is women who have experienced such severe and prolonged denial of their very selves engaging in the struggle to recognise that things can be different, both for themselves as adults and for their children. 'Making something out of very little' is a phrase which frequently comes to mind in the work we do.

Whilst it is vital to recognise this struggle, we must also witness and acknowledge the times when the past manifests itself brutally in the present – when our clients become the abusers as well as the abused. Welldon, in elucidating how the traditional idealisation of motherhood can conceal maternal abuse, writes of how

> our whole culture supports the idea that mothers have complete dominion over their babies; thus we encourage the very ideas [that] the perverse mother exploits. We help neither her, nor her children, nor society in general, if we glorify motherhood so blindly as to exclude the fact that some mothers can act perversely.
>
> (Welldon 1988: 83).

It is the *denial* of the feelings of fury, boredom or even dislike towards children, all of which are part of motherhood, that makes the burden harder for women to bear, and can so often result in these feelings being expressed in secret and perverse ways. By the same token, Winnicott alerted us to the dangers in our clinical work of being unable to recognise and acknowledge our hatred of our clients, of their thoughts and their actions, when he wrote, 'however much he loves his patients he cannot avoid hating them and fearing them, and the better he knows this the less will hate and fear be the motives determining what he does to his patients' (Winnicott 1947: 195). He is reminding us that the therapeutic relationship is by no means immune to continuing the cycle of abuse.

The importance of recognition, for a group of women who may never have felt recognised, is central to the therapeutic intervention we offer. This lack of recognition, coupled with the lack of entitlement to space which many of our clients face, is apparent at the initial encounter between a woman and her counsellor, where again and again women express their surprise at having an uninterrupted space to focus on themselves and reflect on the pattern of their lives. Whilst such an offer of space can be a surprise, it can also be terrifying. Denise is one such client, a young Black single parent, with a history of multiple abandonments in her childhood and abusive relationships with men in adulthood. A bout of severe depression, when her daughter, Pearline, was 2 years old, had resulted in a psychiatric intervention and medication. Denise was separated from her partner, John, although he still visited her, ostensibly to see Pearline. These visits were deeply disturbing to Denise, and occasionally ended in a violent sexual encounter. Her attempt physically to live apart from John was important in allowing her space to think, although, as with many women who have been in violent relationships, the separation deepened her depression, and this was what led her to seek counselling.

There are many disappointing and rejecting maternal figures in Denise's story – the mother who died during her birth; Jamaica, her 'mother country', which she felt both rejecting of and rejected by; Britain, representing the idealised mother, where her adoptive family had migrated in the hope of escaping poverty, and from whom they had experienced the abuse of racism; the Church, which provided a surrogate mother in the form of the home where Denise was born but which then abandoned her to an emotionally unstable mother, chosen for her religious devotion and her desire for a child, rather than for her ability to care for that child. It was hoped that her mother's fragile mental state would improve if she had a child to care for – society's traditional prescription of motherhood as a cure-all for a woman's mental distress. Denise's desire to become a mother herself was tinged with ambivalence. She became pregnant twice before she decided to keep her third pregnancy to term. This was a great achievement as she allowed something to be alive inside her, whilst previously she had felt only deadness and emptiness, although the actual birth of her daughter plunged her into overwhelming feelings of loss. Soon after starting counselling, Denise was faced with what was, for her, a tremendous struggle when she was offered a nursery place for Pearline. Allowing her daughter to separate and grieving over this separation was an enormous step for Denise.

The initial encounter with her counsellor took several weeks to arrange, and there was a real possibility that it would never take place. Denise needed her counsellor to experience what she felt –

that she could never be welcomed in, that she was not entitled to space, that there would always be someone else whose needs came first – whilst at the same time perceiving that she desperately wanted her needs to be recognised and was terrified at the prospect that they would be. It was this desire for recognition, coupled with her conviction that it could never happen, that led to her repeatedly attempting to sabotage the counselling. In initially contacting the Centre she had specified that she wanted to see a Black counsellor, whilst clearly indicating that she expected this request to be refused. It was imperative that her counsellor be aware of Denise's dual and contradictory desires to be both received and to be rejected and thereby wreck the counselling process, and that she knew 'great effort may be required... to catch and keep the patient' (Alvarez 1992: 86) and did not therefore give up on Denise as she repeatedly cancelled and rearranged the first appointment.

When Denise was eventually able to commence her counselling contract, she described how she felt desperate to offer Pearline all the love which she herself had been denied in childhood. Finding it excruciating to witness her daughter's distress or anger, she would desperately attempt to placate her. Denise had become what Raphael-Leff has termed a 'facilitator mother', terrified of her own hatred breaking through (quoted in Parker 1995: 205). Denise gave when she did not want to; she gave by tradition, by rote, and she began to realise how this reflected her behaviour as a little girl who had desperately tried to placate her mother. She had been attempting to deflect her mother's unpredictable and uncontrollable violence. Denise remarked on the similarities between this relationship and those she had evolved with John and her daughter. This insight led to her being able to talk about her fear that she could unleash a murderous rage upon John and Pearline, and how living with and suffering from John's violence had deflected her envious and angry feelings towards her child. Winnicott describes this process thus: 'If, for fear of what she may do, she cannot hate appropriately when hurt by her child she must fall back on masochism, and I think it is this that gives rise to the false theory of a natural masochism in women' (Winnicott 1947: 202).

Many of our clients experience great difficulty in separating out their own and their children's experiences and feelings. Denise would take Pearline into her bed at times when she felt desperately empty and alone. It became clear as the counselling progressed that she found such physical contact necessary to keep at bay a terrifying void. At such times her infantile self became merged with that of her child. It was as if she had become that baby, who felt as though a void had opened up as she lost first one, then a whole series, of parental figures in infancy. The child had become her only link with John and there were times when she left Pearline with him whilst knowing he was drunk and incapable of taking care of her. Denise would return to find her daughter cold, wet and unfed, these physical signs of abandonment accurately reflecting her own childhood experiences.

This conflict of interest between mother and child can be especially hard for the counsellor to bear as 'even in our attempts to focus directly on maternal subjectivity we frequently found ourselves... shifting to the vantage point of the child seeking the need-satisfying mother and then struggling to construct a full vision of the mother herself' (Bassin, Honey and Mahrer Kaplan 1994: 8). Again we have to be aware of the dangers of over-identification with our clients; clients from groups within society for whom a counsellor may share a cultural affinity. In situations where concern for the safety of the child can sometimes push the therapeutic boundaries to the limit, it is vital for us to adhere to a clear vision that we are 'close to our client group... but hate what they do' (Parker, personal communication, 1995). Denise too, struggled with her conflict of interests in her inability to make use of the creche for her daughter, fearing that if Pearline shared the physical territory of the Counselling Centre her own tenuously established sense of a safe space would be annihilated.

Whilst Denise had managed to extricate herself from an abusive relationship with John, there was still a part of her that denied that the abuse had taken place. Several months into the counselling, this awareness suddenly hit her with great force and she was overwhelmed with fear. She fled both John and the counselling relationship, having allowed herself to recognise their importance and therefore the impact of their potential loss. During this period, by allowing Denise to keep in touch by telephone and letter, her counsellor had to actively recognise the client's 'constant and recurring need to be awakened to the peril he is in, and to the human possibilities for him and for his experience when he manages to discover he has live company' (Alvarez 1992: 85). By being alive and active, the counsellor facilitated Denise in the return to her home and to the counselling contract. She became more able to voice her recognition that the 'busyness' of her life during the periods when John was physically abusing her had enabled her to feel alive and had kept her from experiencing an overwhelming depression. Bollas talks about people who experience 'a kind of vacuum anxiety' resulting in a desire to make a connection with the object, in an attempt to feel alive, and explains that by invoking hatred in the object they can feel alive (Bollas 1987: 130). Denise recalled how this manic state of anxiety reflected her overriding experience of childhood when, from morning until night, she was in a constant state of alertness and trepidation, in the midst of a household where her existence was either ignored or punished. In order to survive this traumatic upbringing she had to convince herself that, by allowing herself to be used, she was really in control. The alternative would have been to confront an unbearable well-spring of grief and rage and a terrifying feeling of helplessness.

The conflict of needs, or 'confusion of tongues' as Ferenczi so eloquently describes it (Ferenczi 1933: 164), between Denise and her daughter, as well as the mother's struggle to use the space offered her in counselling, is echoed by the experience of Mary, a 30-year-old Irish woman referred to IWCC by the child guidance unit where her 11-year-old son Scott was being treated. As with Denise, the initial encounter between Mary and her counsellor showed her ambivalence towards counselling and her need to deny and project her abusive self. She arrived for her initial assessment appointment with her partner, Carl, who tried to persuade her that it wasn't worth her spending an hour at the Centre whilst he had to look after her daughter. This appears to have been a crucial moment, when Mary's counsellor was acutely aware of the danger her client was in, as well as recognising how attached she was to this dangerous, yet exciting internal space. It was necessary to convey to the client this recognition, to try and mobilise the part of her which wanted to change. This meant telling her quite unequivocally that the appointment was important, whilst recognising that Mary had already placed her counsellor in the position of engaging in a rivalrous battle with her partner. During the initial part of the consultation, Mary remained unengaged and flippant. Her counsellor commented on how difficult it seemed for her to take herself seriously and her apparent desperation that someone else would do so on her behalf. It was at this point that Mary was able to speak of her grief and her very real fear that she was going mad. Khan speaks of the importance of the analyst mobilising her own will in order to mobilise that of the client in a different way to the way to which she is subject to the will of her abuser (Khan 1979: 208). At this point Mary was living with Carl who would regularly steal money from her and physically abuse her. It was his abusive behaviour, coupled with the return home from a residential unit of her disturbed son, that led her to seek counselling – as if she had been precipitated into an unbearable internal space where she felt her basic sense of self was robbed and denied.

Mary was the eldest of seven children, all born within eighteen months of each other. She always 'felt different' and was the subject of particularly violent punishments by both parents. Mary remembered how she would steal and suck on her baby sister's feeding bottle – a desperate attempt to assuage her uncontained and unacknowledged feelings of need. Stealing and being stolen from, formed a key motif in her life: she would speak with pleasure of other women's jealousy of her ability to 'steal' their men, and gradually it became clear that something had been stolen from Mary herself. When she was 6 years old, she had been sexually abused by a neighbour and subsequently by her father up until the age of 11. Mary had told her mother but was not believed. During her adolescence she became increasingly violent towards her mother who eventually threw her out. Mary became the child Alvarez speaks of, who in identifying 'with the image he feels his parental object has for him... becomes what he feels' (Alvarez 1992: 104).

When she was 15, Mary, feeling and being a plundered object, became pregnant – 'to have something of my own'. The actual birth of her son, Scott, was, she said, 'like being on a butcher's block'. It was as if she experienced the birth as yet another plundering and violation of her body boundary, another rape. The birth of her baby was felt as a violent separation, over which she had no control. She had needed an object which she could control and use for her own gratification, as she herself had been used. Welldon talks about how 'the "nurturing object" can become, under stressful conditions, an object of absolute dominance' (Welldon 1988: 79). This illustrates the importance to Mary of the relationship between inner and outer space and was reflected in her feelings about her home. Towards the end of her counselling contract she was able to start decorating her flat, something she'd 'never bothered with' before, as she felt the space was not hers, mirroring her awakening realisation that she could begin to experience an entitlement to inner space.

Mary had been raped by a friend's husband in her own flat when Scott was a baby. The rape took place in his presence, and for Mary it was doubly traumatic as it awakened memories of the earlier sexual abuse. From this point onwards, Mary experienced Scott's developing selfhood as unbearable. 'He's like my old man', she said, demonstrating how confused the intergenerational boundaries had become for her. Her childhood experience of being both sexually abused and scapegoated within her family began to be repeated with her son. It was as if he had become merged with the abusive adults in her life: 'anger directed toward the husband that turns into violence against the children (which is Medea's anger)' (Doane and Hodges 1992: 49). To Mary, her 2-year-old son had become the rapist, and the anger she felt was directed towards him.

Mary's younger son, Martin, was the favoured 'good' child, whilst Scott became the scapegoat, like Mary, and, like her, his behaviour deteriorated. When he was 9 years old he was expelled from school and was placed in a social services boarding school. Mary voiced her despair about her intense dislike of Scott, how unendurable she found his dependency. One day Scott was found sitting outside the Counselling Centre by a member of staff. It was as if he was desperate to enter a safe 'space' with his mother where he could be recognised and his violent feelings contained. However, when he was invited to sit in the waiting room, he was only able to stay for five minutes before slipping away, perhaps experiencing this intrusion into what he perceived as his mother's space as too frightening. Mary spoke of how much she enjoyed her visits to Scott at his school. She likened it to visiting a male partner in prison. Such a 'prison' was the only place she felt it was safe enough for contact to take place.

Mary experienced her son's desire to be close to her as both persecutory and contemptible: her own desire for connection and recognition was being projected onto him. This mirrored her relationship with her counsellor, where, as she became more dependent, she began to miss sessions, leaving the counsellor to experience, like her client, the frustration of attempting to work with an unreachable object. Recognising that the client would 'depend on the analyst's survival of the attacks, which involves and includes the absence of a quality change' (First 1994: 157), the counsellor wrote each week, recognising Mary's absence and acknowledging also that she would keep open her appointment. Mary, by behaving hatefully, had desperately tried to force her mother to recognise how she felt completely obliterated by her father's abusive use of her as an object for the gratification of his needs, and she, by her absences, now attempted to obliterate her counsellor.

The counsellor's difficulty was to allow Mary to see that it was possible to have an impact on her counsellor; that this impact would not, as in Mary's phantasy, destroy her counsellor or result in retaliation. This was manifested in Mary missing a session each time she began to feel understood by her counsellor, 'spitting out' the good experience before it had a chance to turn bad or disappointing. Mary's battle with herself to trust that she could be accepted emerged when she was eventually able to speak of something that to her had been unspeakable – her wish that Scott would die. Then her memories of the rape would die with him, as would those of her attacks on him as an infant, when she had burned him with cigarettes in an attempt to 'burn out' or obliterate her own vulnerable parts. She needed her counsellor to know how out of control she felt; how unable to protect her son from herself. She voiced her fear that as a result of her violence her son would become like 'those boys who killed Jamie Bulger'. Mary had needed her counsellor to recognise the sadistic part of her, but to allow her to voice it for herself, to know that she needed to be taken seriously, yet not to 'force' this knowledge into her, which would have felt like a repetition of abuse. Mary's desire for revenge for the humiliations and pain of her own childhood was being acted out with her son, as if he could be the object of 'revenge against the denigration she had encountered' (Welldon 1988: 82). In between her first consultation at the Centre and the start of regular counselling sessions, Mary separated from Carl. A new relationship, which she struck up during her counselling contract, proved more supportive, although Mary found herself struggling, for the first time in her life, with an object which was reachable, and which she now recognised she desired to punish and abandon. The reality of the violent and dangerous world in which Mary existed was brought starkly into focus when, half-way into her counselling contract, her former partner, Carl, was arrested for the murder of his half-sister, a friend of Mary's. This shocked and terrified her. She was able to recognise how close to death the denying of her unconscious desire for revenge had brought her. She was able to mourn for her friend, at the same time as mourning for the part of her that had been 'deadened' by years of abuse, and for the breakdown in her relationship with her son. During this time the importance of a safe space where she could think about her attachment to this man was vital to her.

Part of the ethos underpinning the establishment of IWCC was a belief that denial of the impact on society of such issues as race, health and economic deprivation has profound implications for the way in which members of that society are able to fulfil their potential, including the potential for motherhood. With the burden of child care still predominantly placed upon women's shoulders, and with few affordable child-care facilities, the myth of the perfect pair still predominates – the mother perfectly in tune with her infant, and seemingly needing nothing for herself – and is the cause of much guilt amongst mothers. This so-called natural self-abnegation, which informs such concepts as 'good-enough mothering', is far removed from the current real experiences of most women, leading us to question whether it is 'indeed likely that, historically, the selflessness demanded by such mirroring... has ever been attained' (Doane and Hodges 1992: 2). IWCC, by practically and therapeutically recognising that a woman 'needs someone who can let her behave rather in the way she must let her baby behave', provides a thinking recognition of the other (Menzies Lyth 1988: 217). IWCC has striven in its practice to demonstrate that an intra-psychic understanding of development is complementary to what Benjamin (1988: 19) terms 'inter-subjective' understanding, that is, the importance of the subject's place in the world and their need to interact with it, and what Alvarez (1992: 7) terms 'a two-person psychology'. Perhaps being witness to the inner worlds of those mothers who act out their phantasies and abuse their children falls into the category of the 'unthinkable'. What Welldon terms 'society's glorification of motherhood and its refusal even to consider that it may have a dark side' (Welldon 1988: 79) contributes to the continuing imprisonment of women within a sometimes impossible role. Women experience motherhood in myriad different ways, and we need to recognise that motherhood can provide a unique opportunity for a woman to act on her desire for domination or ridding herself of unbearable feelings. A psychoanalytic understanding of motherhood can acknowledge the need for the mother to be 'held' so she can 'hold' her baby. The provision of free and accessible services is an important aspect, demonstrating an effective and active holding.

ACKNOWLEDGEMENTS

We would like to thank the following for their generous and thoughtful contributions in helping us to think about our work:

our clients and colleagues at IWCC; Rozsika Parker; Dr Laurence
Spurling; Professor Lynne Segal; Jean White.

REFERENCES

Alvarez, A. (1992) *Live Company: Psychoanalytic Psychotherapy with
Autistic, Borderline, Deprived and Abused Children*, London: Routledge.
Bassin, D., Honey, M. and Mahrer Kaplan, M., (eds) (1994) *Representa-
tions of Motherhood*, London: Yale University Press.
Benjamin, J. (1988) *The Bonds of Love: Psychoanalysis and the Problem of
Domination*, London: Virago.
Bollas, C. (1987) *The Shadow of the Object: Psychoanalysis of the Unthought
Known*, London: Free Association Books.
Doane, J. and Hodges, D. (1992) *From Klein to Kristeva: Psychoanalysis,
Feminism and the Search for the 'Good Enough' Mother*, Michigan: Uni-
versity of Michigan Press.
Ferenczi, S. (1933) 'Confusion of Tongues between Children and Adults:
The Language of Tenderness and Passion', in S. Ferenczi *Final Contribu-
tions to Psychoanalysis*, London: Hogarth Press.
First, E. (1994) 'Mothering, Hate and Winnicott', in E. Bassin, M. Honey
and M. Mahrer Kaplan (eds) *Representations of Motherhood*, London:
Yale University Press.
Hill Collins, P. (1994) 'Shifting the Center: Race, Class and Feminist
Theorizing about Motherhood', in E. Bassin, M. Honey and M. Mahrer
Kaplan (eds) *Representations of Motherhood*, New Haven and London:
Yale University Press.
Khan, M. (1979) *Alienation in Perversions*, New York: International Uni-
versities Press.
Menzies Lyth, I. (1988) 'Thoughts on the Maternal Role in Contemporary
Society', in I. Menzies Lyth *Containing Anxiety in Institutions*, London:
Free Association Books.
Noonan, E. (1983) *Counselling Young People*, London: Methuen.
Parker, R. (1995) *Torn in Two: The Experience of Maternal Ambivalence*,
London: Virago.
——(1995) Personal communication to the authors.
Raphael-Leff, J. (1991) *Psychological Processes of Childbearing*, London
and New York: Chapman & Hall.
Segal, H. (1995) 'From Hiroshima to the Gulf War and After: A Psycho-
analytic Perspective', in A. Elliot and S. Frosh (eds) *Psychoanalysis in
Contexts: Paths between Theory and Modern Culture*, London: Routledge.
Welldon, E. (1988) *Mother, Madonna, Whore: The Idealisation and Deni-
gration of Motherhood*, London: Free Association Books.
Winnicott, D. W. (1947) 'Hate in the Counter-transference', in D. W.
Winnicott *Through pediatrics to psycho-analysis*. New York: Basic
Books, 1975.

Chapter 9

Parting is such sweet sorrow
The romantic tragedy of a mother–child relationship

Caroline Owens

How, one may ask, does separation of subject and object, of baby and mother, seem in fact to happen, and to happen with profit to all concerned, and in the vast majority of cases? And this in spite of the impossibility of separation? (The paradox must be tolerated.)

(Winnicott 1971: 108)

MOTHER IN MIND

Hannah jumped around excitedly telling me that she could not wait to see the new room. On the way to the room she asked if I would carry the baby doll whose bandage had been removed because she was much better. As I carried the baby doll, Hannah continued to inform me about Peter, who had been to America on holiday and had returned sunburned. 'His back and arms are peeling and they look sore. I'm glad it wasn't me.' She told me that Peter and others had been calling her a predator and that she didn't like it.

When we arrived at the new room, Hannah had a good look around. She asked for some paper and sat down to draw, as though she was familiar with the room. 'I want us to play a drawing game today Caroline, and you have to play too.' I agreed and Hannah explained that we would both have turns at suggesting what to draw. Each would draw the same object and then we would award each other marks out of ten. She suggested a clock, dog, house and candle. She was very stingy with the marks she awarded to me, especially if my picture looked more impressive than hers.

During the time that she was drawing, Hannah told me that she would be getting some tablets from the doctor for her anger. When I asked her to elaborate on this she told me that she did not want to talk about it. 'They are just to help me with my angry feelings, now just stop talking about it or you will make me worse.'

We were thirty minutes in to the session and then Hannah decided that we should play the baby game. (Hannah had been holding the 'baby' throughout and from time to time she would ask her: 'Are you OK, darling?') Hannah then decided that she was too hot and removed her vest and underskirt and put her dress back on again asking me to tie a long bow at the back. Hannah then told me that she had a big argument with her mum that morning and had told her mum that she hoped she and her dad would get a divorce.

I was directed to look after the baby and she (mum) would be going shopping. Hannah told me that the baby was to scream 'her head off' as soon as the mother left the room.

As the baby screamed, Hannah was shouting back at her: 'Shut up, shut up, you are driving me potty.' She told me to make her cry harder and more loudly. As the baby cried more loudly, Hannah came running over to her and hit her on the cheek. 'I told you to shut up, there is nothing wrong with you, I will be back soon.' Hannah told me that the baby was to continue crying and that she (mum) had had enough. She then told me to make her something to eat. 'Make her some spaghetti, she likes that.'

I was then told to feed her with it and that the baby was to protest and spit it out and throw it all over the floor. Hannah smiled, picked up the baby and hit her very hard and then returned her to me to hold, telling me to calm her down.

Hannah then decided that she was the mother who was in hospital dying. The baby and I were instructed to visit her and the baby was told to cry louder than ever when she was told that the mother was dead. As the baby was crying, Hannah was lying on the bed with her eyes closed and was smiling. She then said that they had found a new operation and that the mother came alive again. She instructed me to make the baby give her a big hug. She held the baby tightly to her breast, smiling into her face. Hannah then decided that the baby had been naughty and that she got smacked by the mother. 'That's it, I've had enough of you'; the baby was put on to a chair in the corner of the room. 'Just stay there and you can cry your head off if you like, but you are staying there.' Hannah then said: 'Let's pretend that you are the doctor and I ring you to say that there is something wrong with my baby – and you examine her and tell me that she is dying and there is nothing you can do for her.'

Doctor   Your baby is dying and there is nothing I can do for her.

Mother   Why is she dying?

Doctor   I'm not sure, it might be because she was left all alone to cry her head off.

Mother   It's all my fault.

Hannah looked as though she was about to cry. She was totally absorbed in the role. She lay crying, curled up for a time and it was difficult to tell if she was pretending to cry or if it was for real. She then exhaustedly told me that we would have to bury the baby. She cried even more.

I became the priest who buried her and Hannah collapsed onto the floor crying. After a few minutes she looked at the clock and saw that we had just over five minutes left. Hannah lay in silence for a while. Then she said: 'Pretend we hear her crying from the grave and we dig her up and she is alive again.'

I was instructed to bring the baby to her. She kissed and hugged her. The session had ended, we tidied up. Hannah was quiet. I carried the baby doll downstairs and handed it over to her father as Hannah climbed into the car.

HANNAH

At the time of referral Hannah was 7 years old. The parents' chief concerns were over her constant demands for attention and reassurance. While Hannah had been like this from a very young age, her demands had increased over the eighteen months prior to referral to the clinic. Hannah was wetting in the day and making grunting noises which were becoming a continual source of irritation to the parents. Her parents had become very stressed, believing that Hannah was never satisfied, and they acknowledged that they were finding it very difficult to cope with her. Mother and Hannah were described as being in constant battle, and although Hannah's mother believed her to be a loving child, she found it difficult to understand and tolerate the explosive and angry attacks directed towards her.

Hannah was an only child who had always shown an anxious attachment to her mother, for example, showing reluctance when left at play school when she was 3 years old. Currently she displayed anxiety when left upstairs at night. Her anxieties had become greatly increased since her father had become ill (he was suffering from a debilitating neurological illness).

Presenting as a bossy yet vulnerable child, Hannah was at pains to be good and be liked. She tried desperately to befriend me by staying very close and drowning me with questions about myself. Initially, this was a challenge to my capacity to tolerate and to be compassionate as I experienced being prey to a devouring presence.

During my initial sessions with Hannah I recall feeling extremely frustrated and overwhelmed by her constant demands and limit-testing. This frustration was compounded by the parents' impingements on the sessions as they would often bring Hannah late, miss sessions and want to know exactly what was going on.

I found that my capacity to think had become extremely limited as I became overwhelmed by the vast amounts of material brought and arising from the sessions, as well as their intensity. As I attempted to develop an attuned relationship with Hannah, the therapeutic technique often shifted from child-directed play to a therapy which may be considered to be more analytical in character. I include below sessions where we were moving in and out of child-directed play. Before moving on to the sessions I will explain what I mean by child-directed play.

CHILD-DIRECTED PLAY

Child-directed play is a method I have developed over the years in my work with children who present for therapy. This method of therapeutic work is so called because the child directs the material, storyline and props, as would a director in film or theatre. The emphasis is on the dynamic between child and therapist which is actively explored through the interplay of fantasy, reality and principles of attunement. I have found that by enthusiastically and actively taking up the roles offered to me by children, a richness and depth of exploration of past, present, internal and external experience unfolds.

Many children who come for therapy often appear to be resisting or avoiding difficult issues when they try to engage the therapist in active play. Also, therapists sometimes fear that by engaging in active play they are in danger of contaminating the child's conscious and unconscious agenda. Although I appreciate the inherent difficulties and complexities in any dynamic therapy between child and therapist, I have found the active and dynamic processes to be central to the therapeutic shift whereby children construct, deconstruct and reconstruct their reality.

This approach has been successful in my view because it reflects observed processes and interactions within the the mother–infant relationship (see Stern 1985). For example, both mother and infant are powerful, and the question of who is leading whom is posed. This is an important question. Although the adult may have ultimate responsibility for care of the infant, the quality of care is greatly influenced by what happens between the infant and the mother. Infants are both powerful and vulnerable, as are mothers. The infant's power paradoxically emanates from vulnerability which often manifests as control, so that the mother, for example, often experiences the feeling of being a slave to the infant's needs and demands. Of course, it is crucial for the infant that she has her demands responded to in such a way that she begins to experience a sense of power. It is important also that she has the opportunity to experience and tolerate frustrations. Therefore the mother–infant ability to be with each other includes, paradoxically, being out of step or misattuned, so that two separate selves emerge, gaining their strength from their experience of what is happening between them. In child-directed play the leading and steering shifts between child and therapist as the storyline co-evolves.

TO RETURN TO HANNAH

On my first meeting with Hannah, she told me that her biggest fear was that her mum might leave her. She drew a house which was for sale. Upstairs lived a little girl who was 6 years old. Her parents had gone away and left her. She was very lonely. Hannah, wanted to put the picture on the wall and later decided that she would rather give it to her mum as a present.

Generally, Hannah came across as a creative child who liked rules and was very careful to be clean, tidy and meticulous in her drawings, almost to the point of being obsessive in her attempts not to make mistakes.

As the director in the script described at the beginning of this chapter, Hannah co-created with me a space whereby fantasy and reality were explored. The splitting of 'good' and 'bad', love and hate, self and other were given a stage on which the interplay was acted out. Through this she highlighted very well issues of omnipotence and vulnerability and how they were inextricably linked in contradiction.

On reflection, during this particular session I had observed a different quality in Hannah's communications to me. At times I felt as though I had an adult in the room, and certainly Hannah was engineering direct conflict situations, out of which I became her mother and her 'bad' self in the transference situation.

Although Hannah was prepared in advance for the change of room, her response here was possibly masking extreme anxiety and difficulty with change. This was evidenced by her superficial familiarity with the room and her adhesive activity in the drawing game. Anger resulting from the change of room was directed at me in lowering marks awarded to me in the drawing game. I was denigrated when I produced something 'good' either in games or in linking or interpreting in the sessions.

Hannah projected 'good' idealised aspects into Peter. (Peter was an older boy at Hannah's school to whom she had developed a romantic attachment. Peter not only seemed to avoid Hannah but clearly expressed a dislike of her.) She then felt envious and depleted, and said that she was glad it was not her who went to America and got sunburned. Linked to this was Hannah's communication to me in removing her vest. Perhaps she was indicating that she had got a very delicate skin and was making a plea to me that I should not burn her with my linking and interpretations. Yet she may also have been permitting me to see, and perhaps explore with her, her 'underlayer of skin'. The undressing had been a precursor to talking about the argument with mum.

Hannah's play with the baby doll strongly impressed upon me the intensity of the ambivalent child–mother relationship. It perhaps highlighted the dying part of her baby self, and the fear and wish that another child would emerge as a response to receiving medication. Perhaps the crying and ungrateful baby self could be buried and sent underground, unnoticed and dead, as Hannah in fantasy attempted to kill off the bad self so that the 'good' would 'come alive'. This links to Kleinian theories of guilt and reparation in the depressive position (see Mitchell 1986). Hannah identifies with the mother's guilt. As she announces that it is all her fault, she returns to a psychic and emotive oscillation between these feelings of guilt, omnipotence and destruction which seem linked to hatred of the mother in fantasy.

The play highlighted a degree of fragility, where Hannah's fear of causing damage or being damaged was present in her treatment of the baby. Hannah's baby surely represented the baby part of herself which saw itself as being at the mercy of something unpredictable. It gained control by becoming bossy and predatory. I experienced a feeling of sadness between Hannah and me, as she spoke of her friends who had been calling her a 'predator'. They had so well described what I had experienced of Hannah, and my sadness was both due to their apt acknowledgement of her behaviour and their response to it in running away from and rejecting her. Although I was in touch with the powerless baby, I was also aware of Hannah's attempt to hold on to the adult and parental part of herself, which in this session seemed an immense task for her.

The degree of oscillation and confusion regarding 'death of mother and death of baby' perhaps indicated the internal struggle with parts of self as well as the external struggle with mother. Was Hannah fearful that she would cause mother's death when her mother was absent to her? Had mother threatened Hannah that she was killing her with her naughtiness? In the play, the mother's dying was almost sadistic in that it tortured the baby. I wondered if this extremely ambivalent relationship with mother also indicated that Hannah had not internalised a robust mother: her internal mother was either totally powerful or disintegrating. The deaths in the play were drawing attention to Hannah's omnipotence and the romantic tragedy of this mother–daughter relationship. This unconscious theme appears to be linked to the more conscious reality of the family preoccupation and bewilderment with her father's possible death due to his illness, and indeed with his continued life.

Hannah's wish for her parents' divorce may have related to their developing unity and consistency in managing her, a united couple whom she found it increasingly difficult to tolerate; a couple from whom she had been born. This notion will be expanded further in the following section.

It became apparent to me that Hannah had become quite successful at attacking my capacity to think within the sessions. I often felt unable to reflect back to her the insights I had gained. The emotional and physical space was often filled as I was bombarded with material, and I often felt that my thinking was lacking in clarity. I shall expand upon this in a later section.

THINKING THINGS THROUGH

The following session proved significant also and helped me to gain further clarity about what I thought was going on. On the way to the therapy room Hannah talked about Peter. She said that he had broken his arm in January and he was off school for a long time as a result. As we reached the therapy room Hannah told me that Peter was 11 years old and she was only 8. She said that when she grew up she would like to marry someone like Peter, except that he sometimes did not like her. She decided that she would draw a picture for Peter. She drew a flag which was divided into eight sections. When she had finished the picture she said: 'Caroline, this is not for Peter now, this is for you.' I asked her why she had changed her mind and Hannah told me that her mum had told her that she should leave the boys alone. Hannah went on to say that she was not supposed to hassle the boys. 'Anyway, Caroline, I don't want to talk about it, just be quiet.'

Hannah asked me to hold the baby doll and told me that the baby was upset and that if I was to ask her, the baby would tell me that she didn't know why she was upset. Hannah went on to say: 'She won't eat her food and she just doesn't know why she won't eat her food.' Hannah took the baby from me and said: 'I am the mum and I will put her to bed.' She put her into the cot and wrapped her up in a blanket. She continued to draw for a while and then Hannah told me: 'If the baby wakes up and eats her food, she is OK now.'

Hannah asked for some more paper. She went to the paper tray and lifted the bundle of paper.

H   Caroline, if I take all of this paper, it means that there won't be much left for the other children . . . Who else do you see today, Caroline, who do you see straight after me?

C   You would like to be the only one and have the paper all to yourself, a bit like how you would like to have your mum and your dad, all to yourself. It is difficult to share sometimes.

H   Shut up, Caroline, you're making me worse, I'll tell my mum of you, you are giving me a headache.

C   When you are mad with your mum, you sometimes tell me about how your mum is making you worse?

Giving the impression of quietly ignoring my ideas, Hannah drew a picture of three flowers, a kite and then a flower which was quite separate from the others. Three clouds were drawn in a triangular shape with a tiny cloud in between the two adjacent clouds.

H   Do you have children, Caroline, do you have a family?

C   Perhaps you would like to be my child and perhaps you would like me to be in your family.

H   Shut up, Caroline; stop saying things like that.

C   It seems difficult for you that I think about you, and you want to shut it out, so that you don't hear it, because it makes you feel sad.

H   Look, I wouldn't like you to be my mum, you would be a horrible mum, you would keep mithering me and saying things; I bet that your children think that you are horrible.

[Silence]

H   Just stop it, Caroline.

C   I wasn't saying anything, but I was thinking and I was wondering if you sometimes think that your mum is horrible.

H   Stop it, Caroline! I will tell my mum on you; just stop thinking about it!

C   It seems hard for you that I am in the room with my thoughts and you have to share me with my thoughts.

H   Stop it, Caroline; you make me sick.

[Silence]

H   I'm warning you, don't say another word.

[Silence]

H [shouting] Caroline, will you stop it.

C Are you asking me to stop thinking?

H Yes.

C Do you know what I am thinking?

H No, and I don't want to. What were you thinking anyway and I will decide if I want to hear it or not?

C You told me last week that you hoped that your mum and dad would get a divorce and I was wondering if that is because you find it difficult that they are together. You want each one of them all to yourself, like you want me without my thoughts.

H That's a lie, you are lying, you have made it up. I don't want them to have a divorcement, but I will get rid of you. You make me feel sick.

Hannah said that she would leave if I said another word about it. She climbed into the nest of beanbags, her head cradled between two bags as though they were breasts, and she sucked her fingers on one hand with her other hand over her ear. Silence settled. I told Hannah that she looked as though she was a tiny baby sucking at her mummy's breasts, having her mummy all to herself. Hannah did not comment; she continued to suck. I went on to say: 'I think that it is hard for you, Hannah, that you would like to be all grown up, so that you could marry someone like your daddy and perhaps be your mummy, and so little that you would like to be inside your mummy's tummy again, when your mummy was attached to you and you had her all to yourself.' Hannah lay sucking; she looked at me and pulled another beanbag over her head, so that she was completely immersed in the beanbags and I was unable to see her. There was silence and a voice slipped out: 'I'm not leaving here, Caroline.' I told Hannah that we had five minutes left. Hannah replied: 'You don't have to tell me, I'm not stupid you know. I'm not leaving here, so don't make me.' I replied: 'I think it is hard for you to leave when you look so comfy, all curled up between the beanbags, which are lovely and soft just like being inside your mummy's tummy.' Hannah replied: 'I want to stay for a longer time.'

The time was up and Hannah reluctantly and lazily got out of the beanbags. 'I feel sick, Caroline,' she said, 'I just want to go now, I have to go to the toilet'. Hannah went to the toilet while I held the baby. On her return, she took the baby from me and asked me to carry her books and pens. We went towards her father who was waiting outside in the car. She got into the car and held her baby on her lap and waved as the car drove off.

REFLECTING ON HANNAH

In all the sessions, I had been asked to hold the baby. In one session Hannah told the baby that she would be held every Tuesday by the lady who would look after her. Surely this was Hannah indicating an understanding that she felt the need to be held and contained and that she experienced this within the sessions. She did begin to hold the baby herself in the session described, perhaps because she felt able to, as she had been contained within the session. She could both hold on to her baby self and draw from her internal mother, as at this point perhaps the conflict between love and hate of mother and self had calmed, as Hannah had been 'held in the womb and between the breasts'. She had also had an experience of being held within my mind. Her thoughts, both conscious and unconscious, had been held and handed back to her in a form which despite her anger she was able to tolerate. Being able to hold the baby seemed to indicate a shift towards the depressive position whereby Hannah had found a way of articulating what she felt she had lost.

Over time Hannah showed a capacity to be a compassionate and tolerant mother to the baby, but this was for brief periods and was usually inconsistent. Hannah's observation that 'If the baby wakes up and eats her food now, she is OK now', may have been an indication that she was more able to digest the food provided by links and interpretations, and was taking in some of the 'goodness' of the session and therefore was more able to tolerate the goodness in her own mother. Yet this too was tinged with ambivalence. Spitting out mother's food was also an acknowledgement of her dependency on mother and her difficulty in swallowing this.

Hannah often wanted to take more paper than she could make practical use of. Although she told me to 'shut up' when I commented on her need to have the paper all to herself, her listening permitted me the space to make the link. In fact, I felt generally much more able to think in this session, which may have been connected with Hannah's readiness to digest the food.

In the transference Hannah was perhaps associating having a headache with being made worse by 'motherness'. She immediately split her mother and me by making threats. She was aware that her mother had rung me between sessions and this seemed linked to previous sequences in her presentation whereby any couple, either in internal or external reality, was intolerable to her. For example, Hannah's repetitive and relentless drawings including triadic and dyadic constellations, depicted her struggle. Here the three clouds may have represented the family triangle – a love triangle. The kite perhaps represented Hannah's fear that she was going to drift off away from the parental couple or that they would let her go. The fear may also have included a wish that she could stand alone and separate like the flower.

As I continued to make links, Hannah looked at me with a considerable degree of disdain and her outburst about me being 'a terrible mother' appeared considered and confident. In the counter-transference she had got under my skin and fed in to that part of me which doubts my ability as a mother and as a therapist. The truth was out and I felt exposed, perhaps just as she had felt exposed. I wondered if it was related to her not having me all to herself just as she did not have her mother all to herself. In earlier sessions, Hannah presented as being 'special', and often worked to please me so that I would see how special she was. Here, Hannah was much more in touch with the anger and frustration at not being the only one in her mother's mind and perhaps not being special.

Initially I had thought that her comment on the possibility that her parents might get a divorce was perhaps related to fears arising from external reality. However, it became clearer that, in her fant-asy, if they had divorced, she would have either one all to herself. This was perhaps born out of a fundamental need to have her mother all to herself. This need to remain in partnership with mother was pervasive and generalised to the point that no other couple could be tolerated. In an attempt to understand this I have found Britton's (1985) ideas helpful. He describes a case where his thoughts and thinking are intolerable to his patient, as she experi-ences them as internal intercourse which corresponds to parental intercourse. As Hannah attacked my thinking I was struck by the possibility that she viewed my thoughts as being in partnership with me and therefore as a rival to her.

Hannah could not acknowledge relationships between others and it was therefore intolerable for her to feel that I was communing with myself about her. Perhaps she was experiencing my thoughts and me in intercourse which may have corresponded to her fantasy of parental intercourse. As Britton notes:

> The initial recognition of the parental sexual relationship involves relinquishing the idea of sole and permanent possession of the mother and leads to a profound sense of loss which, if not tolerated, may become a sense of persecution. Later, the Oedipal encounter also involves recognition of the difference between the relationship between parents as distinct from the relationship between parent and child: the parents' relationship is genital and pro-creative; the parent/child relationship is not. This recognition produces a sense of loss and envy, which, if not tolerated, may become a sense of grievance or self-denigration.
>
> (Britton 1985: 84–5)

Although Hannah had been described by her parents as having 'always been a difficult child', they described the difficulties as becoming more marked since the onset of the father's illness. Presumably, this became a time when mother had to give more attention to father. He had taken some of the space in mother's thinking which Hannah had previously occupied. Hannah was almost 5 years old and may have been preoccupied with Oedipal conflicts and struggles. Unconsciously, Hannah may have believed that she had desired her father so much that she had made him ill, like the damaged Peter. She was also unable to ally herself with her mother, who had to go to the rescue of father. Hannah's inability to resolve this, at that time, may have facilitated her regression, as evidenced by her need to climb back into the womb. In this session she lay between the two beanbags, perhaps symbolising the breasts and the two parents. Then she climbed inside, immersed in the beanbags where maybe she could feel she was comfortably in the womb, with her mother all to herself. She could also feel she had interrupted the parents' physical and emotional relationship as Hannah grew inside the mother and between the couple.

Hannah performed many scenarios whereby she was the mother giving birth to the baby and then the mother died in a way that was tortuous to the baby. The emotional intensity of these plays was often tinged with a sexual quality which at times indicated an erotic and romantic relationship between mother and baby. The separation of child from mother appeared to have become catastrophic for Hannah, as she experienced being divided in two, both physically and psychically. This phenomenon is highlighted by Whitford (1991). Drawing from Irigaray's work, she argues that the stress on Oedipus and castration serves to conceal another severance, the cutting of the umbilical cord to the mother. This severance cuts the child off from her beginnings, her conception, her genesis, her birth, her childhood, and she is exiled in the masculine paternal world (Whitford 1991: 25).

In Hannah's world the paternal object is fragile, therefore her separation from mother is, perhaps, even more powerfully experienced as she mourns the death of her first love, her mother. Her plays dramatically portray her pain and struggle to hold a mother in mind, in soul and in spirit.

Hannah's primary presenting problem was a pervasive, adhesive identification which was perhaps precipitated by her position within the Oedipal triangle. We have seen her display an intense love of the mother which, at times, has been to the exclusion of the father. Her preoccupation with dyadic and triadic relationships highlights how the positive and negative Oedipal forms can coexist. The case has highlighted Hannah's struggles as she remains adhesively attached to her mother, and her difficulty in changing her love-object from her mother to her father. I am led towards a consideration of a triangular relationship which was of great complexity and included an exploration of the parents' unconscious desires, the relationship between the parents, as well as an understanding of Hannah's conscious and unconscious experience, all of which has influenced her personality.

As Hannah was able to work through the sadness and loneliness of her feeling of loss resulting from being physically and psychically separate from her mum, in the depressive position she was more able to make reparation. Her play shifted from the concrete towards symbolic and creative expression. It was through her symbolic play that Hannah then moved towards working through some of the difficulties of being separate from her mother. During one session towards the end of the second year of therapy, Hannah told me that she was feeling happy and sad but could not understand why this might be. At the same time she was drawing a picture for her parents. It depicted three fluffy clouds in a triangular configuration, a smaller cloud forming the base point. Underneath, a brightly coloured flower was growing in the sunshine. Inside she wrote: 'To my mum and dad, I have loved you from before I was born, I love you from deep in my heart xx from your little girl Hannah x.' She then went on to tell me that she remembered being a baby in her mother's arms and that although she liked to be held by her father, she preferred mother's arms 'where I was warm and cosy'.

As the relationship between Hannah and me moved towards ending and separation, in one of the later sessions she asked: 'Caroline, please don't ever forget me. Please even remember a couple of my sessions and remember the detail of them. You don't have to remember everything, just remember some of the detail but please don't ever forget me and when my mum dies I know that I will still have her in my mind in a way that I would like you to have me in your mind; it's sort of like we could be with each other even though we are not.'

Hannah was at pains that I acknowledge what I really felt about her, and I think that this was born out of a longing to know what her mother really felt about her. Yet she had embraced my spirit. As she fought for survival, her bravery and despair, precocity and vulnerability, aggression and compassion resonated within me in ways which sometimes felt unmanageable. Yet between us we managed to find meaning. We shared an experience which reflected the intensity and contradictions in her relationship with her mother. Through it all we found ways of tolerating the paradox referred to by Winnicott (1971) and with which I began the chapter.

Hannah need not have feared I would forget her. How could I forget someone who taught me so much? We managed separation as we grew together.

ACKNOWLEDGEMENTS

I gratefully acknowledge the help and support of my supervisor, Mrs Martha V. Smith, Dr. Ruth Simms; whose work with the family has contributed immensely to the successful outcome of this case; Dr Roz Garnish, who kindly read the initial draft; her team collegues and discussion group; and the editors, all of whom in provided support, advice and containment. I also would like to say 'thank you' to Hannah and her parents.

REFERENCES

Britton R., (1985) 'The Missing Link: Parental Sexuality in the Oedipus Complex', in J. Steiner (ed.) *The Oedipus Complex Today*, London: Karnac Books.

Mitchell J., (1986) *The Selected Melanie Klein*, London: Penguin.

Stern D, (1985) *The Interpersonal World of the Infant*, New York: Basic Books.

Whitford M., (1991) (ed.) *The Irigaray Reader*. Oxford: Blackwell.

Winnicott D, (1971) *Playing and Reality*, London: Tavistock.

Chapter 10

Group-analytic psychotherapy
A site for reworking the relationship between mothers and daughters

Sheila Ernst

Group-analytic psychotherapy offers an environment in which developmental processes can be renegotiated with an awareness of the changing boundaries between feminine and masculine. The maternally evocative environment of the group inevitably reflects the social environment through the input of the group members. We shall see how the group conductor's task is to be aware of these social resonances and to incorporate them into an understanding of the unconscious processes of the group.

THE GROUP[1] AS A MATERNAL ENVIRONMENT

Women often imagine that an all-women's therapy group will be a wonderful place in which women can share things, lovingly facilitated by a woman group conductor. For example, in one analytic group for women, the group conductor noticed that this ideal appeared to be realised during the sessions; but afterwards she would be uncomfortably aware that most attention had been given to the men who made the women's lives miserable and little had been said about how they felt about being part of a new group or whether she was making the group a helpful space for them.

Gradually, the group members began to meet each other outside the group for coffee. (This is usually forbidden in therapy groups to ensure that the group is not constrained by the usual social considerations.) Within the group, they discussed alternative therapies, getting anti-depressants from the doctor and the value of 'rescue remedy'. The group conductor, helped by her supervision group, began to analyse her counter-transference (the emotional response evoked in her by the group members usually through unconscious feelings and fantasies), alongside direct messages from the group members. What had gone awry?

She realised that the group members had hidden their anxieties from her at the start of the group, assuming they would be too much for her. Defensively, pretending that they all trusted one another, they projected their negative feelings onto men outside the group. In the group, the group conductor felt comfortable but afterwards she was suspicious. She was overpowered by the sense that she did not need to interfere in the group. It seemed that, in the transference, she was the mother whose capacity to protect her daughters from impingement was in doubt (see Chapter 5's section on relationships between mother and daughter), and the daughters became overtly compliant. Consciously they idealised her, while unconsciously she was denigrated by their search for alternative therapies and by their breaking of the group's rules.

Understanding that a mother–daughter dynamic had overtaken the group, the group conductor could help them to see that she could tolerate her own ambivalence towards her 'group daughters'. This released them from their compliance and they could both articulate their lack of experience of being held and allow themselves an experience of holding within the group.

Both Foulkes (1948), the founder of group analysis, and Bion (1961), another of the early psychoanalysts to work with groups, noted that, in group settings, early experiences of the kind described above were often reproduced. They suggested that, unconsciously, the setting of the group itself evoked a maternal environment which would tend to draw out such deeply repressed parts of group members, originating in the experience of early infancy.

The group conductor can decide how to make use of this facet of group life, depending on her aims. Where professionals want to gain a better understanding of the unconscious dynamics of the organisations they work in, a group setting can be used to give them an intensified experience of the 'primitive' processes at work. The group conductor or consultant does not attempt to facilitate or modify the initial impact of the group but rather to make use of the anxieties generated by interpreting them. The understanding gained in the group can be applied to the work setting. (For gender-aware examples, see Sturdy 1987 and Ernst 1989.)

In a group which aims to provide a therapeutic space for individual group members, the potential of the group for evoking early infantile associations must be dealt with rather differently. The group conductor must take on a task analogous to that of the mother holding the baby (Nitsun 1989); she must make the initial sessions of the group feel safe, recognising and allowing the dependence of the group, rather than 'maintaining a position of therapeutic detachment or making penetrating interpretations' (ibid.: 253). Nitsun is drawing on Winnicott's analogy between maternal care and the analytic setting, and applying it to group therapy. The conductor takes responsibility in the early stages until the group develops what Foulkes called a 'matrix'; that is, the capacity to use its own maternal properties not only to evoke early feelings in the group members but also to process them.

When I am planning a new therapy group, its existence in my mind begins many months before the first group session. I begin to think about the minute details of who the group is for; when it will take place; where it will be; what I hope the group members will gain from it. This planning process is not just a practical matter but involves mental and emotional preparation. There is an analogy to be made with the parents preparing for the birth of a baby; in the process of making the necessary practical arrangements, parents are usually also developing an emotional relationship with the baby who will soon be born. Where the preparation is restricted to the merely practical and represents an avoidance of the emotional aspects of expecting the baby, this may well lead to difficulties when the baby is born. For this reason, group analysis places a great emphasis on the dynamic importance of the preparation for the group, and later on the boundary-keeping activities of the group conductor. It uses the term 'dynamic administration' to convey a meaning which goes beyond the practical.

Thus, to make use of the group's regressive properties for therapeutic purposes, the group conductor must consciously take on the functions of early mothering until the therapy group can manage for itself; moreover, the conductor must be aware that from time to time the group will require this particular kind of attention again. This sense of the group eliciting maternal transferences must be kept in mind by the conductor, particularly in the all-women's groups conducted in an institution like the Women's Therapy Centre, which itself seems to evoke a powerful pre-group transference in its clients.

The example illustrates the importance of being aware of the issue of holding between mother and daughter, if the therapy group is to be used as a space for reworking. It also points to one of the striking things about all-women analytic groups, namely, the powerful counter-transference (Mhlongo Morgan 1987), which can 'suck' the group conductor into what is happening in the group. Often there may be a powerful desire for the group conductor to be the same as the group members, and antagonisms and aggression may be expressed non-verbally through absence and lateness. The group conductor may encounter the same difficulties as the mother has in holding her daughter, where an overidentification and a very strong sense of the infant daughter's anxieties can, if not understood, lead the mother to be overwhelmed by the daughter's anxieties rather than being able to protect her from them. In the group conductor's powerful counter-transference, she may become the overwhelmed, idealised and denigrated mother of the group members' own early lives, rather than the holding presence which they need. Making use of these processes can give the group a special therapeutic potential.

MIRRORING, SEPARATION AND IDENTIFICATION IN THE GROUP

In the next example of a women's therapy group, we see the group members and the therapist negotiating a way of being within the group space which allows the group members to be seen, to feel mirrored by the group, to be able to identify with one another and yet not to feel taken over or 'smothered'. Each woman is trying to find her voice and her space; to do so she needs to be seen and heard, but she fears being too close and intimate lest she loses her fragile sense of self.

The group has five members. Three group members, Gill, Corrie and Ruth are white and English, as is the group conductor. Venus is Iranian and Antoinette is from Mauritius.

The group conductor became aware that she was longing for this group to finish a year earlier than its planned ending and wondered what this counter-transference response to the group might mean. She raised this in her supervision group, telling them about the previous session, which had struck her as being unusual. Only Gill had turned up on time. Ruth, the newest member, was absent and, uncharacteristically, had not left a message. Corrie, who normally looked very drab, arrived late, wearing an unusually brightly coloured sweater. She 'stood out'. Venus and Antoinette also arrived late. Already four out of the five group members seemed to be saying to the group conductor: 'We won't fit in with you and the way you want to do things'. It was almost as if Gill had been selected to be there on time just to make sure that the group could keep going in the midst of the mini-rebellion.

Venus, an art student, arrived at the group, distressed by what had happened in her examination and keen to tell the others about it. She had found it difficult to speak to the examiner. Eventually her tutor took over and spoke for her. As an infant Venus did not find him helpful but felt even more weak and disintegrated.

While Venus was speaking, the therapist was thinking about the origins of Venus's difficulty in 'finding her voice'. Venus must have received very little appropriate mirroring or recognition, since her mother had been mourning the death of Venus's older brother, which had taken place during the mother's pregnancy with Venus. Thus, the therapist could understand why, faced with a testing situation, Venus had not been able to speak. She was still puzzled as to why the tutor's intervention felt so harmful to Venus. It was only through a complex weaving together of Venus's past history and the current experience in the group that the therapist was able to make sense of Venus's response.

The therapist felt wary of jumping in as the tutor had done, and noticed that the other group members were unusually slow in commenting. This seemed to be consistent with the group conductor's general feeling about the group; that she didn't want them for another year. It would be too close. The feeling was confirmed when Antoinette (superficially the brightest and most gregarious of the group members) remarked that she was having difficulty in getting her friends to let her be on her own sometimes. Yet the therapist was left feeling uncertain about the point at which allowing group members the space to reflect would turn into abandoning them to struggle on their own with their difficulties.

What was happening in the group? When Venus described her experience at college, she exposed a shared difficulty: feeling that one is a person who does not have a voice. Venus was expressing something which concerned the group but she became the spokesperson for the group. Her own personal history meant that this recent incident at college had a particularly powerful impact on her as an individual. The tutor's intervention made her feel like a small girl with a mother who did not know how to acknowledge her helplessness, while encouraging her to act as a distinct and separate person.

Other group members demonstrated their need for a degree of separateness in order for each to discover 'who I am'. The therapist also felt that she did not want to be too close to these women; one year of the group would be enough, perhaps two years would be overwhelming and leave them in the state that Venus was in when her tutor took over from her in the seminar. She too was overtaken by the fear that her attempts to provide a holding environment for the group members would arouse a return to early infantile feelings which might be too raw and exposing, too out of control. The other group members had also experienced maternal mirroring distorted to some extent by their mother's depression and despair, and this was highlighted by the extremity of Venus's history. Thus, when the group conductor attempted to offer a mirroring experience it felt terrifying for all the group members, but for Venus in particular, and they feared that this would be a repetition, in which they would be required to respond to the mother/group conductor's distress.

The group conductor understood more clearly what sorts of feelings were being projected into her. She was being made into the dangerous mother who might overwhelm them with her own material. Her sense that she had best withdraw was both an unconscious response to being made into this dangerous figure and an enactment of the group's defensive wishes.

The group conductor was then able to return to the next group session and help them to see what they were struggling with. She could now support each of their attempts to be a person while helping them to articulate their conflicts about finding a position in which they could relate intimately without being attacked or simply overwhelmed. She no longer wanted to close the group early but wanted to extend the period of the group's intimacy.

The group conductor's counter-transference was paramount. Her feelings were powerful, and it was only with her intellect that she knew that simply pulling back from the group was not a solution, that she should not abandon them. She and the group were struggling with the difficulties which arise when the mother's experience threatens to overwhelm the daughter and vice versa. The group conductor was uncertain about how to protect herself and deep anxieties of being literally at risk and open to intrusion were aroused. The group daughters may respond by creating a space around them, but all have to work out a language in which they can talk about the underlying fears and conflicts, so that the space does not simply become isolation but can genuinely be one in which each group daughter can find her own voice.

LEARNING TO 'USE' THE OBJECT IN THE GROUP SETTING

I explained in Chapter 5 about the struggle which needs to take place between the small daughter and her mother, in which the daughter discovers that she can be in total conflict with this person on whom her life has depended and yet that the mother survives the daughter's attack. Thus, the daughter learns that she and her mother have separate existences. When the more aggressive, destructive and hateful feelings which mother and daughter have towards one another cannot be articulated or accepted, then the idea of having a 'straight' fight becomes unbearably tainted with fantasies which make it appear too dangerous to engage in. This is why it is so important to be able to acknowledge maternal ambivalence rather than splitting off certain aspects of the maternal experience, repressing them and having them function as undermining and destructive elements within the unconscious. In the group setting, members become aware of the fantasies that they are bringing into the group and can begin to have struggles between themselves and with the group conductor which allow them to flex their muscles without terrifying themselves.

Powerful fantasies about dangerous and destructive mothers came to a pitch in a session of a mixed group. The group conductor herself was, for a while, caught up in the group fantasy of disaster. At the group's next meeting, the group conductor was able both to see where she had been overwhelmed and to help the other group members to understand what had taken place. Once the outcome of the confrontation had been reduced to more normal proportions, they were able to talk to each other and to the group conductor in a more straightforward way.

This therapy group had five members, four women and a man. They and the woman group conductor were all white and English. The background to the two sessions was of an intense preoccupation with babies, their vulnerability and ambivalent feelings towards them. This was partly because of a pregnant group member, Theresa, and partly because, at another group member's (Jennifer's) work, a family had lost an older child soon after the birth of a new sibling. Theresa was very anxious about the survival of her foetus and her own ambivalence towards the baby, and this introduced ideas into the group about mothers who may damage their own babies. The mysteriousness of the child's death gave rise to the unspoken fantasy that somehow the death might be the parents' fault.

Theresa started the first session by saying that, while her husband was away, she had had to have his favourite cat put down. Although nothing was made explicit, the therapist thought that Theresa imagined her husband blaming her and feared being revealed as the kind of mother who damaged and killed cats and babies. Mary, speaking of a visit to the dentist, depicted herself, in contrast to Theresa, as the victim of dental torture. Both women appeared to want special attention from the group and particularly from the group conductor.

However, the group conductor began to be extremely anxious about a burning smell in the house, to the point where she had to leave the room to investigate. She found nothing. Yet, as if still preoccupied, instead of her usual practice of allowing the group members' response to the situation to emerge, she began to justify her behaviour. She suggested that she had picked up the anxiety about the smell of burning from the group members, especially from Mary. The subsequent discussion was irritable and nothing was illuminated. It was only at the end of the group that the one male group member was able to say that he had felt full of fear throughout the group. After the session, the group conductor felt very disturbed, both by her own behaviour and at the thought that the group members might have been left feeling as troubled as she was.

In the following session the man was away, leaving an all-women group. Mary announced that she would be leaving the group as she had a new job. This sudden leaving plan seemed suspicious, following the disturbing group the week before. None of the other group members commented, alerting the group conductor, since usually when a group member announces that she is leaving, it arouses considerable protest from the group. The group conductor had regained her composure and, instead of interpreting Mary's desire to leave, began to explore it further. Mary said that she had found the therapist leaving the room to chase after a non-existent smell of burning, and then talking about people putting feelings into each other, too closely reminiscent of her mad mother.

The group talked about how frightening it was to have a mad mother. They discussed Theresa's fears about what sort of mother she would be and how frightened she already was about how the baby would control her. Slightly shamefaced, she admitted to wanting a boy. She explained that her mother had favoured her brothers and when they were all teenagers had cut Theresa out completely. This led on to a discussion about how men have a better time and how strange it was to have a gay man in the group who didn't fancy them. The therapist raised the question of their own homosexual feelings. There was a perfunctory response and they began to complain that sex was hardly discussed in the group. Mary spoke about not feeling inside her own sexual experience but being preoccupied with her performance. The group conductor began to feel that she was being asked to join in.

It seemed that Gregory, the one male group member, had been able to articulate something about the frightening nature of the first group session which the others, embroiled in the wordless mother–daughter world, had not been able to distinguish. The women could not talk explicitly, either to each other or to the woman group conductor, about the theme of destructive mothers. The group conductor had sensed the fear of a destructive presence but, instead of being able to think about her counter-transference, she projected the disaster outside the group into the mythical smell of burning. She thought that her anxiety about the burning smell had had something to do with feelings which were being projected into her by the group, but what she did not recognise was that they were projecting their feelings because they could not process them. They had needed her to be the mother/therapist who would protect them by containing their projections. Instead, she tried to explain her behaviour and met with their resistance. Far from being the protective mother, the group conductor had actually been more like the mad mother of Mary's childhood.

In the second group, the group conductor had communicated her ability to take charge of the situation and listen to what Mary and the others were feeling. Relieved, they began to discuss their underlying fears. The crucial change lay in the group conductor's acknowledging the destructive projections, showing the group members that she could both experience such things and think about them. Like the mother Winnicott wrote about, she had been able to survive being destroyed, in fantasy. They then explored some of their feelings about being women, suggesting that mothers are nastier to daughters than to sons, and began to test out the mother/group conductor. Would she be a mother who could accept their sexuality, they had asked implicitly, as they began tentatively to comment on how little sex was talked about in the group. If they became adolescent and talked about sex, would the group conductor join in and become like them?

As the group conductor felt herself being drawn into being one of the girls, she attempted to differentiate herself by telling the group about her holiday dates, which she had not planned to do. The group resented her control over dates and talked about horrible women bosses who don't understand you and are selfish and self-interested.

Without quite realising what she was doing, the group conductor sensed that she must not let herself collapse into an equable discussion with the group members about sex and men, if she was to enable them to work on the mother–daughter relationship. She did something which emphasised that she was indeed the group conductor, if not exactly the boss. This allowed the group members to protest and complain about her in a much less threatening way than previously. She had become a mother who could be struggled with, rather than one so fearful that one cannot speak about her. They had discovered an arena for struggle within bearable limits rather than everything feeling so frighteningly disintegrated or full of unknown smells and dangers.

THE ROLE OF THE FATHER (OR THE 'OTHER' PERSON) IN THE RELATIONSHIP BETWEEN MOTHER AND DAUGHTER

In the previous group, Gregory helped the group to escape from the entanglement of the mother–daughter world by speaking as a male outsider, but he did not attend the next session. This may have been because he was unconsciously aware of the theme of the group; the early attachment between mother and daughter. Sometimes, when this theme emerges within a mixed group, the men will be bored or detached. Perhaps it echoes their own unresolved attachments to their mothers, which may be deeply repressed when they establish themselves as 'boys'. It is useful to be aware of this dynamic in the group because it is one of the ways in which the father, or men who might represent him in the group, can exclude themselves from playing an important part in working through the relationship between mother and daughter. (There are also other reasons to enable men to stay involved at these points, to do with a man's own needs to find his more feminine self, but these cannot be explored here.)

In another mixed therapy group, which met twice weekly, the theme of fathering was used as a context within which three of the women worked on aspects of their relationships with their mothers.

Over a period of several weeks the group was exploring the meaning and the possibilities of relationships with fathers. Although the group conductor was a woman, at times she was seen as the father in the group, the man who had deserted his son, or was present but did not know how to relate to his children. There was Lily's idealised version of her relationship with her father which, as she described it, had sustained her since she had left home twenty years before; she was not sure that she wanted to examine it more closely. Then there was the difficulty of grasping a father's ambivalence about being vulnerable and marginalised.

Meanwhile, Shula, who had been through a long period of depression and had been stuck in an unsatisfying relationship, eventually started a new relationship with a married man. In the group, she was both supported and challenged, eventually becoming aware that the fantasy that she was a little girl, escaping from Mummy into having a loving relationship with Daddy, had to give way to an acknowledgement that she was a woman who was powerful and might be hurting another woman and children in order to get what she wanted. Acknowledging that what she was doing was rivalrous with another woman allowed her to see that to grow up she needed to be rivalrous with her mother. Staying in the group, she could be both rivalrous and still have the group's (mother's) love and support.

At the same time, Lily was able to explore her rejected feelings, particularly those connected to herself as a black baby born to a white mother. She had had a deeply antagonistic relationship to the group therapist, seeing her as the mother whom she could never satisfy (proof of this in Lily's eyes lay in the fact that her mother continued to have more babies). Gradually, as these very painful emotions were articulated, she was able to function positively in the group, showing her strength and risking identifying with the therapist. On one occasion she commented on a yellow jug in the room, saying that the previous day she had felt compelled to buy a jug which coincidentally was yellow. On another occasion she noted the therapist's dress, saying that they were both wearing floral patterns and maybe they were competing.

Tracy began to work on her relationship with her mother in a different way; her pain was connected to not having expressed her own distress in her childhood, but having played a maternal role as the eldest sister, while her parents had their own troubles. Wanting to begin to do something for herself, she started attending a drama class but, having no internal sense of how to work out the conflicts between her drama class and the group times, she simply blurted out her intention to take the course which would mean missing some group sessions at the eleventh hour. Not surprisingly, the other group members were upset by this and felt disregarded. Tracy was able to see how she had replicated her own mother's behaviour in feeling so uncertain about her right to any independence that she just grabbed it, fearing that any discussion would make her waver. She could see both how she was behaving like her mother and also using the behaviour as a way of escaping from her mother's clutches, as if discussion in the group could only ensnare her. Mira Hammermesh, writing about her relationship with her mother, described how she felt when she was leaving home:

> At the door Mother's embrace held me rigid against her, the grip tearing to shreds the resolve to leave. I knew that if I let her hold me one minute more I would never be able to tear myself away from her. Never! Her body was like a magnet, an invisible coil binding our flesh together.
>
> (Hammermesh 1995: 17)

In mixed groups, the mother–daughter relationship needs to be watched out for and attended to by the therapist so that it is drawn out. For instance, when Shula was talking about her new relationship, it would have been easy for both group and therapist to see things in terms of her sexuality and her relationship with her father, and to lose sight of the importance of her working on her envy and competition with mother. For Lily, addressing her relationship with the group conductor/mother was only possible when she had acknowledged the nature and psychic meaning of her relationship with her father. Recognising that there was a strong element of defensive idealisation in it allowed her to look differently at the connection she might have to a maternal figure. Similarly for Tracy, being in a group where there was a strong interactive male presence was helpful, since, in her early life, her father had withdrawn and she had taken up a defensive-protective position in relation to her mother. She needed to believe in the availability of men who could talk so that she could begin to examine her own defensive strategy, rather than having to continue to protect the group conductor and the other women group members from anything which might be construed as remotely destructive.

CROSS-GENDER TRANSFERENCE: WHAT HAPPENS WHEN A MALE GROUP CONDUCTOR IS SEEN AS A MOTHER?

I have emphasised the value both of having men in the group and of introducing the theme of fathering as part of the work on the mother–daughter relationship. I also pointed out that the woman group conductor could be seen as a paternal figure while a male group conductor will often be seen as the mother in the group. The male group conductor may unconsciously want to avoid these transferences, having distanced himself from his early close ties with mother. His interest may lie in attempting to cure the depressed mother of his infancy, as Phillips (1988) hypothesises about Winnicott, rather than identifying with her in the transference. All this needs to be made explicit to help the male group conductor to be aware of such tendencies, so that he does not miss such cross-gender transferences.

In the next example, the therapist had in reality been very burdened both at home and in a new job at work. His wife had had a new baby, and soon afterwards, the family had experienced a painful loss, which had meant him cancelling a group session. There were also a new mother and a new father amongst the group members. Moreover, these two had an outside social connection through their newborn babies. The group felt fragmented; members arrived late and were intense and demanding of the therapist. He felt that he needed to get away from them and had even arranged to take extra time off in the summer, when he would be doing his other work. It became clear that he was feeling like a depressed mother who could not cope with her babies; the more he could not cope, the more demanding they became. Partly for his own personal reasons, he found this intolerable, but he recognised what was happening back in the group and made an interpretation about the group being like Marilyn, the wife of the group member, who had had a baby and been very ill. This released much energy into the group and allowed them to stop reacting to the depressed mother therapist and get on with being stroppy patients.

As the male therapist tried to distinguish between his personal feelings and the group's apparent transference onto him as the depressed mother, he was able to raise the theme in a way he could tolerate. He did not talk to the group about being a 'depressed mother' himself but, by articulating the theme on the group's behalf, he released their energy.

CONCLUSION

I have tried to illustrate the way in which an analytic group can provide a space for work on relationships between daughters and mothers. Firstly, this can happen in the provision of the holding space itself, with its maternal resonances. Later, the possibility of dialogue in the group allows for the subtle and often unconscious renegotiation of the mother–daughter relationship so that the daughter can live her life both supported by 'the internal mother' and able to take support from maternal and paternal others without being overwhelmed.

ACKNOWLEDGEMENTS

Many of the ideas and much of the practice on which they are based were developed at the Women's Therapy Centre, London. I am grateful to the following people who have generously allowed me to draw on our discussions of group-analytic work: Clare Brennan, Molly Chan-Williams, Andrew Donovan, Michael Fischer, Inge Hudson, Camilla Johnson-Smith, Sheila Ritchie and Margaret Smith. I would like to thank the group members of many groups for their contribution to this chapter.

NOTE

1 For those readers who are not familiar with group-analytic therapy I include a brief account of how such groups work. A group-analytic therapy group consists of about eight members selected by the group conductor, who meet, once or twice weekly at a regular time and place, for an hour and a half. It is the conductor's (or therapist's) task to enable the group to become an entity, to form what is termed a 'group matrix' or to grow a sort of skin around them such that the group begins to have an existence of its own. Within this group space, the individual group members, each bringing their own past histories and fantasies, begin to explore their interactions with other group members. Gradually they come to see each other and the conductor without this extra 'shadow'

or role from the past and have more choice about how they relate in the present. The group conductor maintains the flow of associations between group members, not leading the group, but facilitating their communication through understanding the transferences and her own counter-transference. She also maintains the boundaries of the group and takes on the responsibility of being the therapist for each individual group member.

REFERENCES

Bion, W. (1961) *Experiences in Groups*, London: Tavistock.

Ernst, S. (1989) 'Gender and the Phantasy of Omnipotence: Case-study of an Organization', in B. Richards (ed.) *Crises of the Self*, London: Free Association Books.

Foulkes, S. H. (1948) *Introduction to Group-Analytic Psychotherapy*, London: Heinemann.

Hammermesh, M. (1995) 'I Love my Mother, but', in J. Goldsworthy (ed.) *Mothers by Daughters*, London: Virago.

Mama, A. (1995) *Beyond the Masks: Race, Gender and Subjectivity*, London: Routledge.

Mhlongo Morgan, A. (1987) 'Working with Women in Groups', unpublished lecture, Institute of Group Analysis, London: General Course.

Nitsun, M. (1989) 'Early Development: Linking the Group and the Individual', *Group Analysis*, 22 (3): 249–61.

Phillips, A. (1988) *Winnicott*, London: Fontana.

Sturdy, C. (1987) 'Questioning the Sphinx: An Experience of Working in a Woman's Organization', in S. Ernst and M. Maguire (eds) *Living with the Sphinx*, London: The Women's Press.

Chapter 11

'I wouldn't do your job!'
Women, social work and child abuse

Brid Featherstone

INTRODUCTION

'I wouldn't do your job!' For many social workers this sentence captures the ambiguity with which they are viewed. On the one hand, such a statement can reflect the feelings of those who see social workers as carrying an unbearable load in coping with the distressing things people do to each other. On the other, it can reflect the sentiments of those who feel they would not do the job because of the distressing things they believe social workers do to others.

This chapter looks at an area of social work which is particularly charged; that of mothers' involvement in the abuse of their children. It is primarily concerned to address the issues that are raised for women social workers in such circumstances. Surprisingly little attention has been paid to the fact that when mothers neglect, beat, suffocate, kill or sexually abuse their child/children, it is often another woman (who herself may be a mother and almost certainly has been a daughter) who is involved in investigating, assessing and working with her and her family. The chapter is primarily concerned with the issues which are raised for women social workers, although it recognises that these are also pertinent for others, such as police officers and doctors. While I recognise that there are important issues raised for male professionals in such circumstances, these are beyond the scope of the chapter.

In their dealings with abusive mothers I will be arguing that women social workers are hampered by poor theoretical tools and their location in organisational contexts which are often unhelpful. Despite the apparent polarisation of key theoretical approaches, the most common of which is that between psychological and sociological explanations, they are often united by fantasies of an essential harmony between mothers and children which, if disrupted, needs explanation and can be restored. These fantasies also pervade writings on the relationship between women social workers and service users and lead to assumptions that workers can 'empower' or 'remother' their needy clients. Workers carry these inadequate theoretical tools into public sector organisational contexts which are manifesting increasing defensiveness and the inability to face both external and psychic reality (Obholzer 1994). Consequently, such workers find little space or support to understand and explore the complexity of the relationships they encounter. One consequence has been a retreat from theory, as social work in the area of child abuse has become constituted as a pragmatic activity which is concerned with following procedures and government guidelines. Linked to this has been the development of approaches which are primarily concerned with allocating parental responsibility rather than seeking causes (Dale *et al.* 1986).[1] This process is often not located within an interrogation of the relationship between power and responsibility and, as a result, can lead to punitive and authoritarian practices. Such practices flourish in a climate whose dominant characteristic is one of disappointment, a disappointment which flows from earlier fantasies of harmony.

I will be arguing for the importance of utilising understandings of ambivalence (Parker 1995) to move social work away from such theoretical blind alleys. Furthermore, I will argue that this could help with understanding relationships between social workers and mothers and the organisational contexts in which they are located.

THEMES FROM THE LITERATURE

The literature on child abuse is concerned with four key issues: its status as a social problem; why it happens; how it should be treated; and finally, how it should be managed. In terms of the first issue there is a considerable literature devoted to exploring the political processes by which certain kinds of activity become defined as abuse and the interests that particular definitions serve (Parton 1985). This approach is often linked to Foucauldian-inspired analyses such as that of Donzelot (1980). Donzelot analysed the transformations that took place in the late nineteenth century around the emergence of a certain set of discourses which were interrelated via their common concern with the family (Parton 1990a: 11). He described a very important change from government of the family to government through the family.

> In the nineteenth century...there develops an alliance between the medical profession and hygiene technicians and the mother of the bourgeois family. She it is who is to become the ally of the "experts", the educator of the family and the executor of the experts' orders. Donzelot sees in this process an alliance of moralizing philanthropy and promotional feminism...The children of the bourgeoisie under this benevolent maternalism, grow up in "supervised freedom"; for the working class it spelt increased *surveillance*.
>
> (Barrett and McIntosh 1982: 97; emphasis in original)

Donzelot's approach has been widely criticised by feminists such as Barrett and McIntosh (1982) for the way it appears to mourn the passing of 'traditional' families which were based on the power of the father and its apparent blaming of women for 'inviting' the experts in. His analysis has also been used to support arguments which are opposed to social control. Such arguments often appear to imply that clients' problems are not real but figments of social work biases (Gordon 1986). They also ignore the possibility that men, women and children may have different interests and needs in relation to state intervention. As Gordon (1986, 1989) has argued, the relationship between women and welfare workers has been quite a complex one, with women using welfare workers in their own and their children's battles against male violence and abuse. Children have also used such workers to defend themselves against parental power relations. There continue, however, to be ongoing tensions between acknowledging that children get hurt and abused and the role of the state in identifying and controlling certain kinds of families as abusive.

In terms of exploring 'why' child abuse occurs and how it should be treated, I am primarily concerned with developments since the 1960s, when child abuse was 'rediscovered'. The initial focus was on child physical abuse and neglect. Bowlby and Kempe are usually recognised as having influenced significantly the direction of policy and practice on child care and child abuse in the UK. Bowlby's work stressed the importance of secure attachments for children and posited abuse as the most extreme expression of a parent's incapacity to form an attachment. His work led to a series of papers and studies on child abuse, early separation experiences and the consequent failure to develop bonding (Lynch and Roberts 1977; Argles 1980).

The role of mothers was seen as central (Martin 1983). Even when the focus was not on actual mothers, mothering practices were seen as key. For example, Steele (1976), a close associate of Kempe, who was the originator of the term 'the battered baby syndrome', argued that during his many years of working with parents who neglected or abused their children, he and his associates had come to believe that the basic ingredients of their behaviour originated in the earliest part of their lives and arose predominantly from their own lack of empathic mothering (ibid.:13). This, he argued, was more significant than any other factors such as gender, socio- economic status or living conditions.

The therapeutic perspectives of Kempe and his associates promoted the development of long-term nurturing relationships between workers and clients. The aim of such relationships was to satisfy unmet dependency needs on the part of parents who abused their children and to provide them with reparenting which, in practice, meant remothering. Care and control functions were separated out, as were legal and therapeutic tasks. The local authority became responsible for any necessary court proceedings (thus becoming the authoritarian father?) leaving Kempe's workers free to concentrate on forming purely therapeutic relationships with the parents. Such relationships were developed in 'ideal circumstances', in the sense that the work was well-resourced and supervised and adequate training and research facilities were provided (Dale *et al.* 1986).

Walkerdine and Lucey (1989) provide an understanding of the context in which these perspectives were formed. They note that a strong movement in the 1940s and 1950s tried to produce a possibility of social reform through the agency of the mother. In order to support reform, the pessimism of Social Darwinism was countered by an environmentalism which, instead of stressing aggression and war, emphasised the possibility of social reform through love and nurturance. The project of social democracy created natural mother-love as an object which was to be the bedrock of its policy (ibid.: 141).

Within the child abuse literature this environmentalism was compounded by the preference accorded the work of Bowlby and the relative lack of attention paid to the work of Melanie Klein. Her work did not lend itself easily to optimism about harmony between mother and child, but rather drew attention to the splitting, envy, loss, depression and reparation involved in mothering (Sayers 1991a). However, it has largely been ignored in the social work literature.

The work of the early theorists and clinicians came under fire largely as a result of three developments: radical social work, the 'rediscovery' of child sexual abuse and a number of child abuse scandals which resulted in child deaths. The radical social work movement of the 1970s was scathing about the predominance in social work of what were seen as approaches that focused on emotional difficulties and that pathologised individuals and their families. There was an explicit rejection of psychoanalytic and psychodynamic approaches (Pearson, Treseder and Yelloly 1988). Radical social workers argued that problems caused by class divisions, such as poverty and poor housing, were being neglected. From a perspective broadly sympathetic to this tradition, Parton (1985) launched an influential critique of the child abuse literature, a critique he later acknowledged was gender-blind (1990b). He argued that this literature was dominated by a socio-medical model which conceptualised child abuse as a disease which could be diagnosed and treated. His focus moved attention to the role of the state and professionals as definers of social problems and also highlighted the importance of exploring issues such as poverty, poor housing and unemployment. As he later acknowledged, he did not address the issues raised by sexual abuse as distinct from physical abuse. The feminist approaches to physical abuse developed during this period were also concerned to move away from the focus on individual mothers and argued that contributions such as those of Kempe and Steele ignored the constraints of motherhood and the pressures which were placed on mothers to cope (Graham 1980).

The rediscovery of sexual abuse was largely due to the work of survivors and feminist organisations. They were concerned to address a number of key points: that sexual abuse occurs in all classes and is not correlated with poverty or stress; that it is not the result of individual men's pathology and women's collusion but is linked to wider systems of male domination and power; that the construction of masculinity is key to understanding its occurrence and that, if women do sexually abuse, it is usually as a result of their coercion by men. These analyses became highly influential among feminist social workers. For a summary of some of the dominant perspectives see *Feminist Review* 1988.

Feminist social work approaches in the main shared with the radical social work literature a hostility to psychoanalytic understandings, and so social constructionism became the key to understanding relationships between mothers and children. In the frequent assumption that the answers lay in improving the social conditions under which mothers mother or in eliminating male power, a fantasy of essential harmony between mothers and children was reproduced which ironically shared some of the premises of work such as that of Bowlby (Walkerdine and Lucey 1989).[2] This was compounded by the preference given to large-scale universalist theorising and the consequent failure to produce local, contextual analyses which explored everyday negotiations between men, women and children (Wise 1990, 1995; Featherstone 1994). Postmodern critiques of how knowledge is produced and acquired have until recently had a limited impact upon feminist social work theory. There has, therefore, been little attention paid to developing approaches which acknowledge that all theories and theorists are themselves located within power–knowledge relations and have marginalising and regulatory effects.

Partly influenced by a number of highly publicised child deaths in the 1970s and 1980s and reflecting the wider sense of disappointment with earlier approaches, Dale *et al.* (1986) took a less rosy view of families and the role of professionals. Whilst they did not develop a clear theory of what constituted dangerousness, they argued that there were dangerous families where children were abused as a result of triangular relationships between perpetrator, victims and partners who failed to protect. They argued against the goal of developing long-term therapeutic relationships or providing reparative parenting or material help and for the importance of individuals and families taking responsibility for their lives. 'The role of the therapist becomes less to do with changing others, than to do with providing the context for people to make their own changes' (ibid.: 10). It was also felt to be important that workers did not hive off legal responsibility to others, thus perpetuating the splitting of professionals into good and bad or arguably authoritarian fathers and caring mothers, as was the danger with earlier approaches. A team approach was used and it was felt to be imperative that both parents were engaged with, irrespective of who had carried out the abuse, as the dynamics between them were vital. Their work was clearly based on aspects of family therapy theory and practice.

Critiques of this work have centred on its gender-blindness, not-ing that its theoretical assumptions ignored power imbalances between mothers and fathers and contributed to mother-blaming by exploring interactional dynamics between both parents. How-ever, by trying to engage both parents, it did attempt to rectify some of the difficulties of other work where fathers were marginalised or absented themselves (for example, in the early work of Kempe and his associates[3]) or were seen as the source of abuse and, therefore, as beyond therapy and in need of punishment (for example, in feminist approaches). Furthermore, Dale *et al.* avoided the difficulties posed by those approaches which focused exclusively on mothers, seeing them either as the sole source of the difficulties or as the child's main source of protection.

The difficulties, in my view, lay not in their focus on both parents and their assumption that the interaction between them is vital, but in their failure to think through the relationship between power and responsibility. In assuming mothers and fathers had equal respons-ibility for their children, they did indeed ignore power imbalances and arguably contributed to overly punitive practices. However, the understandable anxiety on the part of feminists to avoid mother-blaming has resulted in an equally problematic tendency to assume that women carry no responsibility. More recent feminist work within the family therapy field has begun to address this issue in important and exciting ways (see Burck and Speed 1995), and I will be looking at this in a later section.

As I indicated previously, the literature on child abuse has been concerned with four key issues: its status as a social problem; why it happens; how it should be treated; and finally, how it should be managed. The latter concern has arguably very often been at the forefront of professional concern. As Hallett (1989: 10) notes, there is a long tradition in British public administration of using commit-tees of inquiry or tribunals to resolve difficult issues of public policy and to investigate scandals, tragedies or other matters which are causing concern. Some inquiries, such as that into the death of Maria Colwell,[4] have been more influential than others. This particu-lar inquiry dealt a catastrophic blow to the confidence and percep-tions of the newly emerging social work departments (Bamford 1990). Such departments, set up in the optimistic days of the early 1970s, appeared to promise an invigorated, expansionist and integ-rated vision for the profession. However, the avalanche of media attention paid to the inquiry into Maria's death gave voice to and encouraged the deepest misgivings about social work competence, training and communication systems. Highly publicised inquiries in the 1980s have continued the focus on the management of child abuse systems. One such inquiry, that into the death of Jasmine Beckford (London Borough of Brent 1985), did broaden out to focus on why child abuse occurred, but did so from a positivist perspective which implied that there were clear-cut risk factors which could be identified via a diagnostic process (Parton 1986). Another, that into the death of Tyra Henry (London Borough of Lambeth 1987), addressed issues in relation to race and cultural stereotyping but, in general, the focus of these inquiries has been on how to deal with abuse rather than why it occurs. The most famous example of this was the inquiry into the handling of sexual abuse cases in Cleveland,[5] which was primarily concerned with how to manage the investigation and treatment of child sexual abuse but which did not go on to explore why sexual abuse occurred (Campbell 1988). Furthermore, as Reder, Duncan and Gray (1993) argue, in a systematic review of over thirty inquiry reports into child deaths, the reports produced tended 'to focus over-much on matters of professional responsibility and accountability at the expense of analysing the psychological aspects of the cases' (ibid.: 4). For example, there have been repeated recommendations for improved communication systems between agencies but little analysis of what psychological factors might impede communication in cases of abuse.

Alongside concerns about the adequacy of procedures for detecting and dealing with abuse there have coexisted concerns about authoritarian practices which intrude into 'innocent' families. The Children Act (1989)[6] was an attempt to balance these concerns. To a large extent it redefined social work as an activity which is regulated by law, thus handing over to the courts 'this work which inevitably deals with the most painful and anxiety making of situations and which...build[s] on the most private nuances and subtleties of interactions between members of the family group' (Valentine 1994: 84). This attempt to bring certainty into the process is scarcely surprising given the nature of what is being dealt with. It also feeds into a continuing tendency, which has been to divide off those who are at high risk or who are dangerous from the rest, thereby consigning abusiveness to the margins of society.

Social workers are therefore operating in a climate which is defensive and adversarial. Organisational developments and changes may be compounding their difficulties. Obholzer (1994) has noted that the current situation in many public sector organisations militates against their ability to face both psychic and external reality. An ability to face these would mean not only

> agreement about the primary task of the organisation, but also remaining in touch with the nature of the anxieties projected into the container, rather than defensively blocking them out of awareness. In order for a system to work according to these principles, a structured system for dialogue between the various component parts is necessary.
>
> (Obholzer 1994: 173)

This is not happening in many public sector organisations with the increased divisions between managers and practitioners and increasing fragmentation between services.

Furthermore, as Woodhouse and Pengelly (1991) point out, social workers in public sector organisations operate as the end-point for referrals from other agencies, thus literally becoming the containers of the anxieties of others. They cannot gatekeep, thus they are unable to draw the kinds of boundaries that are drawn by non-statutory agencies. If a child is in danger they must investigate, however overworked they are or the system is. They visit people in their homes and are often unable to set up structured appointment times in less emotionally charged territory. There are often few appropriate facilities for carrying out structured work. Furthermore, they usually occupy a range of complex and contradictory positions in relation to their clients: for example, acting as advocates on their behalf in relation to other agencies, and as mediators, reporters to the courts and counsellors/therapists.

WOMEN WORKING WITH WOMEN

Women continue to constitute the majority of frontline social work practitioners whilst, despite the increasing number of women entering first-tier management, the upper echelons remain male dominated. Women also predominate amongst those who request, receive and mediate service provision in the child-care area. The recognition that social work is an activity carried out in the main by women with women has led to a degree of interest from feminists and to the development of a growing literature. This literature, like the more general feminist literature, is marked by ambivalence, omissions and gaps (Flax 1990). For example, there has been little research carried out into the views of women service users or of women workers or their perceptions of each other. Furthermore, as Wise (1995) points out, there has been little written about what actually happens in everyday working interactions. This is in contrast, for example, to the psychotherapy literature where case studies are regularly used to illuminate particular aspects of the therapeutic process. There is little written by feminist practitioners, and a considerable amount is written by those who have never been practitioners at all. Furthermore, the literature remains largely untouched by the developments signalled by postmodernism and poststructuralism. Consequently, the ability to reflect on its own status or effects and to review its own orthodoxies, particularly in the areas of violence and abuse, remains underdeveloped.

Within feminism generally there has been a high degree of ambivalence about the state and women's relationships with the state, whether as workers or as clients, and consequently about women's relationship with power. While feminists have campaigned for the enactment and enforcement of state legislation against violence by men, there continues to be anxiety that this may result in women being ruled by a form of public patriarchy rather than by individual men. Consequently, effort has been devoted to the development of services which are led by women and not located in the statutory sector. The invoking of state powers, whilst recognised as necessary and of great importance both historically and currently for women and children, has also been regarded with unease because of its differential impact on particular groups of women and men, for example black women and black men (see, for example, Mama 1989).

Women social workers therefore pose uneasy questions for feminism both because of their power over other women and because their work brings them into contact with women who are abusing those more vulnerable than themselves, namely, children. In general, power relations between women have more usually been explored in the wider literature in terms of class, 'race', sexuality and disability, and these discussions have been the source of distress, discomfort and anger as well as resulting in richer, fuller and more creative analyses. There has been little discussion about the kinds of power relations in which women occupy positions of authority over other women as employers or where they are authorised to use certain kinds of legislative powers against each other. There has been a limited discussion about the situations in which women abuse their power over children. Women social workers cannot avoid questions about power and are embroiled on an everyday basis in actively working through concrete questions about how power relations work in practice among men, women and children.

To some extent, the feminist literature on social work tries to bypass the question of power by constructing an appeal to women social workers which emphasises their identities as women rather than as social workers. Consequently, it is scarcely surprising that White (1995), in a recent piece of research which was designed to test the resonance of this literature for women social workers, found that some of the social workers studied pointed to a 'duality of existence' in which distinctions between feminism and social work were made. Feminism was 'as much, or more, a private or semi-public identity, as it was a public cause or a route into alternative forms of social work' (ibid.: 155). Arguably, feminism was seen as relevant to the rest of their lives but much more problematic when considered in the context of their work as statutory social workers.

Key injunctions of the feminist social work literature have been that women workers and clients share a common experience of victimisation at the hands of men, and that women workers should therefore like and value their women clients and cultivate ways of working which maximise opportunities for reciprocity and sharing (Hanmer and Statham 1988). The commonality of women's experience is the starting-point for feminist practice and, in this view, the diversities that exist can be incorporated and transcended (White 1995).

Wise (1995) has pointed to the abstractness of much of this writing in relation to the problems social workers face, and also argues that it is vital that women social workers acknowledge and use the powers they possess in order to protect those who are less powerful, such as children. She points, for example, to the difficulties posed by a woman who leaves her children consistently unattended or with unsuitable babysitters. It may be possible to like and value her, but it is impossible to avoid questioning her ability to protect her children who are more vulnerable than she is.

A further question which workers face on an everyday basis is how responsibility should be allocated. As we have seen, Dale *et al.* (1986) were criticised for their view that responsibility for abuse was shared by both parents. Feminists have consistently argued that by not differentiating between women's and men's actions, mother-blaming is encouraged.

In practice, these questions become exceedingly complex. It is indeed true that women are oppressed by individual men and wider systems of domination. However, does this absolve them of any responsibility for their children's welfare? Whilst it is unacceptable that women have been burdened with sole responsibility for their childrens' welfare, surely the answer does not lie in absolving them of any. Not only is that kind of reversal unhelpful in advancing our understanding of difficult questions, but it does not help individual women to think through the issues for themselves. They want and need to know what they could have changed in order to safeguard their children. Furthermore, their children often need to know. Henessy (Gorell Barnes and Henessy 1995) describes how important it has been for her to acknowledge her mother's 'responsibility' in her father's abuse of her. As Burck and Speed (1995: 3) note, 'Challenging "women blaming" should not lead to exonerating women from any responsibility at all, as this would diminish women's sense of effectiveness and agency altogether'.

There is a growing acknowledgement, then, of the need to develop more contextual understandings (Wise 1990, 1995) and of the need to be able to hold macro understandings about cultural tendencies to blame mothers alongside micro understandings about the complexities and variations in women's and children's own experiences (Burck and Speed 1995). There is also some recognition of the need, identified by Gordon (1986, 1989), to move away from the victimisation paradigm which has dominated feminist scholarship in relation to violence and to acknowledge that women's involvement in abusive activity cannot be read simply as flowing from their victimisation at the hands of men. However, this recognition is, in my experience, still much more common among practitioners than among theoreticians, and this discrepancy is both a symptom of, and contributes to, the gap between the two.

Moreover, whilst further thinking on the range of ways in which women meet each other in the child protection system is vital, difficulties will remain if the relationship between women workers and their clients continues to be seen as one which can be constructed rationally and consciously within the context of feminist guidelines on sisterhood.

Feminist psychoanalytic writings have indicated how relationships between women evoke powerful feelings which are not amenable to political imperatives about correct behaviour (Orbach and Eichenbaum 1987). There is also a considerable body of writing on the issues that may come up in the therapeutic process. Lawrence (1992) and Sayers (1991b) have used this literature to explore some of the implications for women social workers working in the area of child abuse. I will look at this in the next section.

WOMEN WORKING WITH WOMEN: PSYCHOANALYTIC INSIGHTS

Lawrence (1992) summarises some of the main formulations of feminist psychoanalytic thinking which she considers to be useful and relevant to child-care practice and to women working with women. She argues that women, like all subordinate groups, learn that they can only achieve influence through men. This means that they are primarily concerned with pleasing men rather than meeting their own needs. Indeed, they experience their very survival as being dependent upon their ability to please. She bases her analysis on the work of Orbach and Eichenbaum who argue that the essential difference between men and women lies in the mother–daughter relationship before the father becomes an important figure in the constellation (the pre-Oedipal period).

Under patriarchy, in Lawrence's view, it is the task of the mother to induct her daughter into the role of second-class citizen and to encourage her to meet the needs of others. She learns to be a carer and not to expect to be cared for. This developmental trajectory has particular implications for women's relationship with anger and hatred, emotions which are forbidden them.

Lawrence (1992) points out that women social workers share a common developmental experience with their women clients. One of the ways in which women learn to put their own needs aside is by dealing with them vicariously, for example, through looking after other people. Instead of being in touch with their own unmet needs, women are often inclined to look for others even more needy than themselves, and to make themselves feel better by taking care of them. Women who go into social work or other caring professions are often the good daughters; daughters who from an early age were reliable and helpful, not causing anxiety or distress in their own mothers and in fact repressing the messy, envious, upset, childish parts of themselves. She asks women social workers to consider their attitudes to needy women: 'As "copers" ourselves, do we unconsciously blame and punish women we see showing that they have difficulties' (Lawrence 1992: 45). It is quite possible, she argues, for women workers to make the mistake of expecting too much of their needy clients, much as abusing parents often do of their children. For the woman social worker, working with very needy distressed women can present a similar challenge to that of mothering a baby daughter.

Whilst there is much of great value in Lawrence's analysis, there are some difficulties with the theoretical premises on which she bases it. Firstly, some important criticisms have been made of the work of Orbach and Eichenbaum which are relevant here. Bar (1987) highlights two theoretical problems which also pose questions about therapeutic technique. One relates to the status of the unconscious and the other to how 'need' is to be understood. She argues that by posing the unconscious as the intra-psychic reflection of present child rearing and gender relations, Orbach and Eichenbaum defuse its radical potential. Furthermore, she argues, their conception of need is flawed, and that needs can never be known purely in themselves but only through their relationship to pleasure and unpleasure: 'the infant suckling at the mother's breast is not only satisfying a need, but experiencing something sensually pleasurable, which sets it off on its journey of differentiation' (Bar 1987: 230). She also uses the work of Dinnerstein, who in turn was deeply indebted to Melanie Klein, to argue that human development is prompted through loss rather than the satisfaction or frustration of need and that life thereafter is a deeply ambivalent experience. Bar's conclusion is that, as a result of their flawed conception of need, the aim of Orbach and Eichenbaum's therapy would appear to be to remother the woman client, in the sense of making good what the client was deprived of in her childhood.

Lawrence's work is important in moving debates away from rational, voluntaristic notions of women social workers being able through acts of will to like and value women clients. She also opens up some important insights into why women may become social workers and the problematic implications this may have for their relationships with women. However, by staying within Orbach and Eichenbaum's focus on need, she misses out on such key questions as the significance of loss and ambivalence. Consequently, her analysis implies that if women social workers were made psychologically aware, they would be able to meet their client's needs.

Writers such as Flax (1993) have asked whether the tradition of which Lawrence is a part, in promoting the therapist as a good mother, sustains harmful and unrealistic fantasies in women clients of the perfectly attuned partner. She asks whether a certain level of frustration may not actually be necessary in order to facilitate the development of self-reflection and a realistic sense of agency. Orbach and Eichenbaum (1993) too have acknowledged criticisms of the way in which, in their earlier work, they offered themselves to women as containers and therefore as the one who could tolerate and survive, thereby perpetuating the idealisation of woman (mother) as object.

Women social workers working in area offices potentially occupy a multitude of contradictory positions in relation to their women clients: as therapist, wielder of statutory powers, advocate, negotiator, mediator. Some of these positions clearly conflict. For example, if a worker recognises that a woman is very fragile and needs to be contained, she also has to remain aware of the need to assess how her behaviour is impacting on her children. Furthermore, unlike a therapist who frequently does not have a legal mandate, she (the social worker) has little choice about whether to challenge a woman's behaviour. Social workers are compelled to do so if it is seen as endangering a child's safety. The following example highlights vividly some of the dilemmas.

Margaret had previously sexually abused a child in her care. Consequently, her own children were made the subject of court orders, although they remained living with her. She received ongoing therapy from a woman therapist who did not have statutory responsibility for the case, whilst a local authority social worker (also a woman) held the statutory responsibility. This meant looking after the children's welfare, convening the statutory reviews and liaising with all those involved. The therapy revealed that Margaret had endured a shocking childhood of sexual, emotional and physical abuse. When she revealed that she was experiencing sexual feelings about a child, the professional network was thrown into disarray. Was she a threat to her own children? Did they need to be removed? Workers found themselves becoming stuck in fixed positions whereby she was produced as either a victim or a victimiser.

Further difficulties arose for the social workers as a result of the level of hostility and anger Margaret directed at them, which led them to feel persecuted and overwhelmed. Relationships between workers and between agencies became fraught as they were positioned by her and each other as respectively good and bad. In this case an all-woman network struggled both with concrete dilemmas to which there were no clear-cut answers and with their need for approval and fear of hostility from each other. Although it is a feminist orthodoxy that women are more usually inclined to seek approval from men, in my experience this is not so. Women's disapproval of each other can be experienced as particularly painful. This is especially so when women are involved in deciding whether or not a woman can care for her own children. One of the most painful aspects of this case was that there was no 'right' answer. Nobody could say for certain whether or not she was a sexual threat to her own children. Nobody could say whether it was better to leave them at home with her while she completed the therapeutic work she required or whether it was better to remove them and give her space to work on her own pain. No-one knew whether that would make her feel even more persecuted and anxious that she had lost them. Transference and counter-transference relations were central to the processes operating here and yet they have received relatively little attention in either the social work literature or the feminist literature.

TRANSFERENCE AND COUNTER-TRANSFERENCE

Transference is the process by which the client transfers feelings applicable to a previous relationship into the present one... whilst counter-transference can be defined as the feelings which arise in practitioners towards their clients, either in response to the transference, or as result of the (usually unresolved) personal issues which the practitioner brings to the relationship.

(Erooga 1994: 207–8)

Sayers (1991b) has addressed how transference and counter-transference relations can operate in child abuse cases. She argues that feminist attention to sexual inequality has resulted in greater awareness of the possibility that there may be differences in the reactions of men and women workers to child abuse, particularly child sexual abuse. She documents the kinds of feelings which can arise for both men and women workers when men have sexually abused.

Little attention has so far been paid to the counter-transference reactions which can be stirred up when, for example, it is the mother who sexually abuses rather than the father. With Margaret, the level of distress engendered in the workers was higher because she was a woman and a mother. This was partly because much worker time and support had been offered her. There was ongoing therapeutic involvement and there was also a strong identification with her victimisation. Moreover, her own anxiety about her feelings triggered corresponding anxieties in some workers. Could they also abuse? In bringing some of them in touch with their own feelings about desire and violence, Margaret became the focus of considerable anxiety.

There has been little space for women to talk about or express their feelings in these areas or to explore their transference and counter-transference reactions. A small body of literature has grown up in relation to men, but this literature has little resonance for women, implying as it does that feelings of sexual excitement elicited in the course of therapeutic work are linked to dominant notions of masculinity. For many women, the lack of general recognition that they too can experience a range of reactions to hearing about abusive behaviour or desires may leave them feeling isolated and freakish. Furthermore, it can lead them, as workers, to avoid particular areas of work or alternately to seek them out and to try to cope alone with quite terrifying feelings.

More generally, Orbach and Eichenbaum (1993) have noted some of the difficulties which can arise in the counter-transference between woman therapist and client. They argue that women therapists are challenged to do two things. One is to become the non-subject mother, the woman who is lost inside a relationship, powerless, dissatisfied and feeling helpless. The second is to maintain enough of oneself as a subject. They argue that the latter is needed by both the client and the therapist. For if the therapist remains merged she is useless both to the client and to herself. Although one part of the treatment is to hear the despair, the anger and the hopelessness and to survive the feelings of victimisation and powerlessness of the mother, another, arguably more important, aspect is to maintain oneself as a subject.

This is vital for women social workers. Because feminist social work theory has concentrated so much on hearing the hopelessness and the victimisation, it sometimes has difficulty with the latter task. This is thrown into particularly sharp relief where cases such as that of Margaret are encountered where a woman has suffered appallingly herself but is or may be a danger to others.

There are of course other situations where workers cannot allow themselves, or are unable to bear, the feelings of victimisation expressed by their women clients. This may be because they feel they themselves had to fight to escape or because they are frightened of being submerged in someone else's pain. Jilly's case highlights some of the complexities here. She had one child whom she frequently requested should be removed permanently from her. Jilly had suffered from depression for many years and presented as very flat and uncommunicative with all the workers involved. Approaches ranging from feminist therapy to medication had been used in the past. Her little boy's father had disappeared many years previously and she had no current partner. The circumstances surrounding her child's birth and his behaviour on an everyday basis were not traumatic or difficult. She just felt she did not wish him to live with her and said this frequently in front of him. Her social worker (a feminist woman) became aware of feeling utterly furious with this woman and wanting to punish her for her 'selfishness'. To her horror she found herself using stigmatising language to denounce her and to distance herself from her. She found herself unsympathetic in relation to the woman's depression and finished sessions feeling powerless and angry.

Through supervision the social worker was able to acknowledge her counter-transference and explore her responses, recognising that these were linked to her own feelings of fear about becoming depressed herself. A number of significant people in her family had suffered with depression and it was something she both despised in them and feared might happen to herself. Furthermore, her anger was linked to her envy of this woman for being able to say what she wanted despite the possible shame that might accrue to her for so doing. The social worker also became aware that she was identifying with the child and his feelings. However, as the work went on she found herself developing punitive feelings towards the little boy and indeed became aware of a very strong desire to hit him physically. These feelings were terrifying to her and led her to avoid spending any time with him on his own and eventually to transferring the case to another worker. Although there was some space to talk about her feelings towards the mother, there was none to talk about her feelings towards the child. That a woman social worker might want to hit a child, particularly a vulnerable child who had been rejected by his mother, was quite literally unthinkable. In retrospect, she recognised that her identification with him had thrown up feelings of pain and vulnerability for her which she found very anxiety-provoking and for which unconsciously she blamed him.

WORKING WITH AMBIVALENCE

Rozsika Parker has written in this volume (Chapter 2) and elsewhere (1995) about the importance of acknowledging maternal ambivalence: 'the experience shared variously by all mothers in which loving and hating feelings for their children exist side by side' (1995: 1). She distinguishes between manageable and unmanageable ambivalence. Manageable ambivalence, she suggests, can play a creative role in mothers' and children's lives leading to an increased capacity to think and act. The capacity to think is probably the most important aspect of mothering. If a mother regards her child with only hostile feelings or with untroubled love, she will not focus on the relationship because she will be unaware of what is missing. She argues that it is the troubling coexistence of love and hate that propels a mother into thinking about what goes on between herself and her child. However, as we live in a culture that is itself ambivalent about maternal ambivalence, the guilt stirred by the recognition of ambivalence can become overwhelming and immobilising. 'Society's wariness of maternal ambivalence ... provides a context which inflates maternal guilt, rendering ambivalence at times unmanageable' (ibid.: 21).

It seems to me that the exploration of maternal ambivalence between mother and child could have helpful consequences in two important respects. Firstly, it could move the child abuse literature away from the idealisation involved in fantasies about an essential harmony between mothers and children and the subsequent denigration which can accompany the disappointment when such fantasies do not work. Secondly, it could be used to understand the difficulties that arise in relationships between women workers and their women clients and enable the development of more informed practices in relation to such difficulties.

An acknowledgement that ambivalence towards maternal ambivalence extends right through organisational and working relationships might help us to understand the continuing failure to allocate space, time and resources to the work and the workers. Acknowledging this ambivalence would encourage demands for the space to think and reflect, and for the psychologically informed supervision which is so necessary.

Despite the gaps in the literature, it is clear from practice that social workers encounter manifestations of unmanageable maternal ambivalence on a fairly frequent basis, and they develop ways of working with mother and child which ensure as far as possible that the child receives a good-enough experience and is safe. However, there are times where the failure to recognise what is happening can have tragic consequences and these are, of course, the cases which receive media attention. The press coverage of the Celia Beckett case focused once again on the failures of the profession. Celia killed one daughter, left another brain-damaged and poisoned her youngest before welfare professionals became suspicious. As Beatrix Campbell and Michelle Paduano (*Guardian*, 11 November 1995) wrote, 'For years as successive disasters befell her three girls, Celia Beckett had escaped detection, cocooned by the conventional wisdom that mothers know best and that mothers must mother'. I would add that what was also at play was the comforting fantasy that all mothers love their children, or if they do not they can be helped to do so.

Jackie's case exhibited similar features with a less tragic outcome. She had killed a child previously and had been imprisoned for this. Upon her release from prison she remarried and subsequently became pregnant. It was agreed by the professionals involved that she could keep this child because, it was argued, she had been under considerable social pressure at the time of the previous murder. This social pressure was now removed. Jackie's baby was born, a beautiful and healthy baby girl. She was very well cared for physically but appeared to be constantly ill. She had frequent admissions to hospital, initiated by her mother, for breathing problems. Furthermore, as she got older her mother spoke in increasingly disparaging ways about her and in front of professionals talked of wanting to 'kill her'. These sentiments are relatively familiar to child-care workers, and whilst not dismissed are accepted as echoing the inevitable difficulties of mothering. They are, however, charged when they emanate from one who has already killed. Jackie also found it difficult to hide her feelings about workers and appeared only able to cope with those who were approving or sympathetic. She found the smallest degree of criticism unbearable and would use her considerable skills to invalidate those workers of whom she did not approve.

Changes in the social work personnel involved with the case provided opportunities for Jackie both to try and negate any critical comments they made and to compare them unfavourably with previous others who had been in her eyes 'good workers'.

When the child was again admitted to hospital (her twentieth admission in a few months), the social workers decided to remove her from her mother's care. She flourished with foster parents and had no further admissions to hospital.

Jackie professed to love children and offered her services frequently as a babysitter to neighbouring mothers. She was adamant that the frequent admissions to hospital were evidence of her concern for her child's well-being. Indeed, one of her defining characteristics was her co-operation with professionals and her reliability in attending appointments. Social workers are accustomed to recalcitrant and frequently hostile clients who seek to avoid them if at all possible. Therefore such co-operation can be a relief and can lull workers into a sense of security in relation to how the case is progressing. However, as Jackie played out her ambivalence in her interactions with workers by seeking them out, asking their advice and then becoming quite hostile towards them and/or her child, the workers were forced to think more carefully about what was happening.

Clearly, mothering provided some relief for Jackie's psychic distress by providing her with legitimate access to professionals who could potentially hear and recognise this distress, but mothering was also a key contributor to this distress in that it involved rearing an actual child with all the demands that entailed. Because the workers concerned were able to disentangle to some extent what was happening and to recognise that this was unmanageable ambivalence, they were able to take action that probably saved the child's life. This does not mean that all sorts of feelings were not raised for them in the process: feelings of anger, distress and discomfort. In particular, there was tremendous anxiety about getting it right and not just responding in a defensive and punitive way by removing the child.

CONCLUSION

'One of the characteristics of the postmodern moment is the proliferation of subject positions that historical individuals occupy'
(Kaplan 1992: 182). A range of writers have addressed the consequences of this proliferation for men and women and the relations
between them and have analysed issues such as sexuality and men's
violence (see, for example, Weedon 1987; Hollway 1989; Frosh
1995). A key characteristic of the period is anxiety, as one would
expect in a period of intense transition. This anxiety can be dealt
with by rigid defensiveness and authoritarianism. For example,
violence by men to women could be read in such a way currently.
Alternatively, men may choose new ways of behaving and thinking,
ways which are uncertain and tentative (see Frosh 1995 and this
volume, Chapter 3).

Kaplan (1992) argues that there has been a paradigm shift that is
more specific than the global postmodern one; a shift which encompasses different forms of anxiety and is to do with childbirth and
child care no longer being viewed as an automatic, natural part of a
woman's life-cycle. 'Whereas in earlier periods... the sound-image
"woman" was congruent with "mother"... things are now more
complex' (ibid.: 182). She suggests that this is an important source
of current anxieties, both for men and women.

Social workers find themselves managing, mediating and reckon-
ing the implications of changing generational and gender relations
for individual households. This is not new. As Gordon (1989) noted
from her historical study of family violence, battles within families
were often about competition for scarce resources, both material
and emotional. Such battles were intertwined with wider societal
disputes about the rights, responsibilities and expectations of men,
women and children. Women social workers have found themselves
in paradoxical positions in relation to such battles; often at the
forefront of change, they have also sought to roll back the process
of change. Grappling with the consequences of enormous changes
in their own lives has sometimes left them depleted in relation
to others. Their own ambivalence about mothering has seldom
been allowed public expression either by themselves or the men
who have, in the main, managed them. Acknowledging such
ambivalence in themselves and others would be an important step
forward in fostering a climate of thought and reflection. Furthermore, it would name and make visible the everyday practices in

which they engage and which seek to mitigate the effects of unmanageable ambivalence.

ACKNOWLEDGEMENTS

I would like to gratefully acknowledge the help provided by Lyn Romeo, Jillian McCormick and Wendy Hollway in helping me think through the ideas contained in this chapter.

NOTES

1 Carol-Ann Hooper (1992) has noted the existence of what she calls a 'child protection discourse' in contemporary welfare organisations. Such a discourse is primarily concerned with allocating parental responsibility. I am focusing on Dale *et al.* (1986) as their work is the most explicit expression of this discourse. It is, however, implicit in a wide variety of other publications and discussions.

2 Walkerdine and Lucey are making a more general point than I am as they are addressing feminist theory in general and object relations in particular. I am arguing that their point is also relevant to feminist social work and this will become very obvious in later discussions of work such as that of Marilyn Lawrence (1992).

3 Workers at Denver House, where Kempe's therapeutic perspectives were pioneered, were very anxious to get men involved but they were largely unsuccessful. This is one of the key criticisms of their work by Dale *et al.* (1986). My point here is that their focus on mothering meant they were unable to identify a clear role for fathers, so, despite their exhortations for them to be involved, there was no clear focus for men.

4 In January 1973 Maria Colwell died of injuries inflicted by her stepfather. As there had been statutory involvement by social services, a public inquiry was held. This proved a turning-point in media and public attitudes towards social workers.

5 In 1987, between the spring and early summer, 121 cases of suspected sexual abuse of children were diagnosed by two paediatricians, Dr Higgs and Dr Wyatt, in Cleveland in the north of England. The interventions of the local MP Stuart Bell and irate parents resulted in the holding of a judicial inquiry in October 1987. See Campbell (1988) for an account.

6 The Children Act (1989) was the result of years of consultation and deliberation and brought public and private law together in relation to children and families. It was generally welcomed by all the political parties and a majority of those involved in child-care organisations. It has been argued by some commentators to mark a move from a discourse which was largely socio-medical to one which is socio-legal, thus placing the courts and the law at the centre of decision-making about children. (See Parton 1990a for an account of this view and of the background to the legislation.)

REFERENCES

Argles, P. (1980) 'Attachment and Child Abuse', *British Journal of Social Work*, 10: 33–42.
Bamford, T. (1990) *The Future of Social Work*, London: Macmillan.
Bar, V. (1987) 'Change in Women', in S. Ernst and M. Maguire (eds) *Living with the Sphinx*, London: Virago.
Barrett, M. and McIntosh, M. (1982) *The Anti-Social Family*, London: Verso.
Burck, C. and Speed, B. (1995) 'Introduction', in C. Burck and B. Speed (eds) *Gender, Power and Relationships*, London: Routledge.
Campbell, B. (1988) *Unofficial Secrets, Child Sexual Abuse: The Cleveland Case*, London: Virago.
Campbell, B. and Paduano, M. (1995) 'Smother Love', *Guardian Weekend*, 11 November 1995.
Dale, P., Davies, M., Morrison, T. and Waters, J. (1986) *Dangerous Families: Assessment and Treatment of Child Abuse*, London: Tavistock.
Donzelot, J. (1980) *The Policing of Families: Welfare Versus the State*, London: Hutchinson.
Erooga, M. (1994) 'When the Personal Meets the Professional', in T. Morrison, M. Erooga and R.C. Beckett. *The Assessment and Treatment of Sexual Offenders*, London: Routledge.
Featherstone, B. (1994) 'Victims or Villains? Women who Physically Abuse their Children', in B. Featherstone, B. Fawcett and C. Toft (eds) *Violence, Gender and Social Work*, Bradford: University of Bradford.
Feminist Review (1988) Special issue, Spring, no. 28.
Flax, J. (1990) *Thinking Fragments: Psychoanalysis, Feminism, and Postmodernism in the Contemporary West, Oxford*, University of California Press Ltd.
——(1993) 'Mothers and Daughters Re-visited' in J. van Mens-Verhulst, K. Schreurs, and L. Woertman, (eds) *Daughtering and Mothering, Female Subjectivity Re-visited*, London: Routledge.
Frosh, S. (1995) 'Unpacking Masculinity: From Rationality to Fragmentation', in C. Burck and B. Speed (eds) *Gender, Power and Relationships*, London: Routledge.
Gordon, L. (1986) 'Feminism and Social Control', in J. Mitchell and A. Oakley (eds) *What is Feminism?*, Oxford: Basil Blackwell.
——(1989) *Heroes of their own Lives: The Politics and History of Family Violence, Boston 1880–1960*, London: Virago.
Gorell Barnes, G. and Henessy, S. (1995) 'Reclaiming a Female Mind from the Experience of Child Sexual Abuse: A Developing Conversation between Writers and Editors', in C. Burck and B. Speed (eds) *Gender, Power and Relationships*, London: Routledge.
Graham, G. (1980) 'Mothers' Accounts of Anger and Aggression towards their Babies' in N. Frude (ed.) *Psychological Approaches to Child Abuse*, Guildford: Billing.
Hallett, C. (1989) 'Child-abuse Inquiries and Public Policy', in O. Stevenson (ed.) *Child Abuse, Public Policy and Professional Practice*, Hertfordshire: Harvester Wheatsheaf.

Hanmer, J. and Statham, D. (1988) *Women and Social Work: Towards a Woman-centred Practice*, London: Macmillan.

Hollway, W. (1989) *Subjectivity and Method in Psychology*, London: Sage.

Hooper, C-A. (1992) 'Child Sexual Abuse and the Regulation of Women: Variations on a Theme', in C. Smart (ed.) *Regulating Womanhood: Historical Essays on Marriage, Motherhood and Sexuality*, London: Routledge.

Kaplan, E. A. (1992) *Motherhood and Representation: The Mother in Popular Culture and Melodrama*, London: Routledge.

Lawrence, M. (1992) 'Women's Psychology and Feminist Social Work Practice', in M. Langan and L. Day (eds) *Women, Oppression and Social Work: Issues in Anti-discriminatory Practice*, London: Routledge.

London Borough of Brent (1985) 'A Child in Trust: Report of the Panel of Inquiry Investigating the Circumstances Surrounding the Death of Jasmine Beckford', London: London Borough of Brent.

London Borough of Lambeth (1987) 'Whose Child? The Report of the Panel Appointed to Inquire into the Death of Tyra Henry', London: London Borough of Lambeth.

Lynch, M. and Roberts, J. (1977) 'Predicting Child Abuse: Signs of Bonding Failure in the Maternity Hospital', *British Medical Journal*, 1: 624–6.

Mama, A. (1989) 'Violence against Black Women: Gender, Race and State Responses', *Feminist Review*, 32, summer: 30–48.

Martin, J. (1983) 'Maternal and Paternal Abuse of Children: Theoretical and Research Perspectives', in D. Finkelhor, R. J. Gelles, G. Hotaling and M. Straus (eds) *The Dark Side of Families: Current Family Violence Research*, California: Sage.

Obholzer, A. (1994) 'Managing Social Anxieties in Public Sector Organisations', in A. Obholzer and V. Z. Roberts (eds) *The Unconscious at Work: Individual and Organizational Stress in the Human Services*, London: Routledge.

Orbach, S. and Eichenbaum, L. (1987) *Bittersweet: Facing up to Feelings of Love, Envy and Competition in Women's Friendships*, London: Century Hutchinson Ltd.

——(1993) 'Feminine Subjectivity, Counter-transference and the Mother/ Daughter Relationship', in J. van Mens-Verhulst, K. Schreurs and L. Woertman (eds) *Daughtering and Mothering: Female Subjectivity Revisited*, London: Routledge.

Parker, R. (1995) *Torn in Two: The Experience of Maternal Ambivalence*, London: Virago.

Parton, N. (1985) *The Politics of Child Abuse*, London, Macmillan.

——(1986) 'The Beckford Report: A Critical Appraisal', *British Journal of Social Work*, 16(5): 511–30.

——(1990a) *Governing the Family: Child Care, Child Protection and the State*, London: Macmillan.

——(1990b) 'Taking Child Abuse Seriously', in Violence Against Children Study Group (eds) *Taking Child Abuse Seriously*, London: Unwin Hyman.

Pearson, G., Treseder, J. and Yelloly, M. (1988) 'Introduction: Social Work and the Legacy of Freud', in G. Pearson, *et al. Social Work and the Legacy of Freud: Psychoanalysis and its Uses*, London: Macmillan.

Reder, P., Duncan, S. and Gray, M. (1993) *Beyond Blame: Child Abuse Tragedies Revisited*, London: Routledge.

Sayers, J. (1991a) *Mothering Psychoanalysis*, London: Penguin.

—— (1991b) 'Blinded by Family Feeling: Child Protection, Feminism and Countertransference', in P. Carter, T. Jeffs and M. K. Smith (eds) *Social Work and Social Welfare* (Yearbook 3), Milton Keynes: Open University Press.

Steele, B. (1976) 'Violence within the Family', in R. Helfer and C. H. Kempe (eds) *Child Abuse and Neglect: The Family and the Community*, Cambridge: Ballinger.

Valentine, M. (1994) 'The Social Worker as "Bad Object" ', *British Journal of Social Work*, 24(1) February: 71–87.

Walkerdine, V. and Lucey, H. (1989) *Democracy in the Kitchen: Regulating Women and Socialising Daughters*, London: Virago.

Weedon, C. (1987) *Feminist Practice and Poststructuralist Theory*, Oxford: Blackwell.

White, V. (1995) 'Commonality and Diversity in Feminist Social Work', *British Journal of Social Work*, 25: 143–56.

Wise, S. (1990) 'Becoming a Feminist Social Worker', in L. Stanley (ed.) *Feminist Praxis: Research: Theory and Epistemology in Feminist Sociology*, London: Routledge.

—— (1995) Feminist Ethics in Practice', in R. Hugman and D. Smith (eds) *Ethical Issues in Social Work*, London: Routledge.

Woodhouse, D. and Pengelly, P. (1991) *Anxiety and the Dynamics of Collaboration*, Aberdeen: Aberdeen University Press.

Index